Neil Willis continues his writing career, further to *One Year On My Hundred* and *Songs From The Mansion House Garden*, with *The Men With No Names*. Written as poetry and prose it allows him more expression to the reader. Ever opinionated, ever thought-provoking, he can seduce you into softness before spelling a harsh reality, but leaving you wanting a little bit more.

*The Men With No Names* is to be read from first page to finish to get the full storylines passing through the book. These are four-fold: the life of the seated man, a brief touch-history of black people's lives, the small town with a democracy hill for debating, and the world of peculiar people.

With lots of love to my darling wife, Emma. x

Neil Willis

# THE MEN WITH NO NAMES

AUSTIN MACAULEY PUBLISHERS™
LONDON * CAMBRIDGE * NEW YORK * SHARJAH

Copyright © Neil Willis 2022

The right of Neil Willis to be identified as author of this work has been asserted in accordance with section 77 and 78 of the Copyright, Designs and Patents Act 1988.

All rights reserved. No part of this publication may be reproduced, stored in a retrieval system, or transmitted in any form or by any means, electronic, mechanical, photocopying, recording, or otherwise, without the prior permission of the publishers.

Any person who commits any unauthorised act in relation to this publication may be liable to criminal prosecution and civil claims for damages.

A CIP catalogue record for this title is available from the British Library.

ISBN 9781398465640 (Paperback)
ISBN 9781398465657 (Hardback)
ISBN 9781398465664 (ePub e-book)

www.austinmacauley.com

First Published 2022
Austin Macauley Publishers Ltd
1 Canada Square
Canary Wharf
London
E14 5AA

# CONTENTS

The Seated Man, 9

White Man's Land of Freedom, 31

The Seated Man 2, 43

The Man Who Held The Sky, 47

The Seated Man 3, 61

Upon Speakers' Hill, 63

The Lives of Women, 65

The Seated Man 4, 79

The Centennial Rock, 83

La Bête Noire, 85

The Seated Man 5, 95

Groupers' Hill, 99

Cricket Pitch Kid, 101

The Seated Man 6, 109

Protesters' Hill, 113

The Running Man, 117

Seated Man 7, 123

Banners' Mount, 129

The Lives Of Men, 131

The Courthouse, 141

Seated Man 8, 147

The Jail Cell, 157

The Seated Man, 163

The Future Vision, 173

Remembrance Hill, 179

Repeated Man, 183

**The Seated Man**

It was apple-bobbing season. On the edge of the river were the single cupped-hand-sized falls that were stolen by the autumn wind. Over-ripe, the former curves of bright green, that once glimpsed light to sheen, had now rotted to yellow, then to dark brown after the branch-jump down. Aged-skins were as leathered-faces, akin, scarred by the last bump. The few that looked as new were saved by the tarpaulin of leaves that duveted the trees' surround.

The ground was a camouflage netting that undulated over raised roots that clambered, to then amble, as a cover to woodland paths. The late teatime sun sheered through each branch to highlight the rougher edge of the trees' barks; that were part of an assault course for squirrels to scamper. With their legs prostrate-stretched, they climbed cautious, suspicious, then to glimpse the trees' girths, as statues to spy. In a split second they were scared to fast-clamber to the tops, then again feed, as though escaping hostages, freed.

Where had they gone to?

Through the browned-green, no longer seen.

Hidden bandits, that should wear a nose-covering bandana, you could hear them screech-cry, but not see the thick of thieves that pried.

They, head-first, quick-traipsed the shady side of the beech.


**The Squirrels**

The ground of hazelnut falls and browned acorns,
A treasure hunt through picking leaves,
They scampered.
Quick head to turn,
As though filled with guilt,
Then again, slick as thieves.

Their humping rumps with plumed-tails, adorned,
The light tickles each fine-stranded hair
As though lamp-lit;
Colours of burnt,
So quick they would retreat,
As though masters of deceit.

Watch the band of thieves;
Covered-noses by handkerchiefs,
The ovalled gains to their claws,
Acting beyond nature's laws,
Brimming their winter hampers.

Each gloried nut tooth-tampered after the fall,
A shaker to their hair-growth ears.
The smiling teeth
Of the known thief,
With nose that twitched the honed jewel.
The prize, paw-to-breast-held, as their treat.

They're scuffling beyond where police-eyes, once saw.

Evidence, woodland-buried beneath the leaf fall-floor,
The scratcher of the peat-like layer,
Smug in his thought,
And never caught.
The arched flurry of disbanded earth,
To then scurry from the criminal scene.

No tracks to the leaves.

Seen to the bright of sunlight,
But then invisible to the shade to hide.

Admire the tricks up their sleeves ...
Disappearing in a moment, brief,
... Of the shy bandana-clad-clique of thieves.


As the autumnal leaves fell like soft rain, one could now get a view through the treetop canopy to the cloud-patched, oil-painted sky, that moved left to right. Each cumulus, distanced to the next, with white, trifle mould-curved stepped edges, that caught the setting blush as they floated west to the sun, but with darker grey, flat head brush-swept following sides.

The edging feathers of wide-to-glide red kite birds were caught to higher bluster of wind, bending as though raised flaps to an aeroplane's wings. One could see the ruffling to their breasts, as they did their best to muster; to be head-strong for the onslaught that the later storm would bring. Parading anchor-head, dark grey cumulonimbus towers blooming, as threatening, marched as a baying army from the easterly-skies.

The kites as crosses, were nose-diving as bladed-propeller wartime planes, to the field carcass of a rabbit life, lost. Their beaks tearing at its cheeks, to then again rollercoaster upwards to plateau as wind-high spies. Of little sound, were the stolen, air-swept, hunting cries.


**The Red Kites**

Spreading, were the barbuled-feathers,
That were feebled to the looming weather.

Baying, were hovering crosses to the skies,
Planes as though a tipped-wing display,
Patterned to glow-filled clouds' sides,
That blushed to autumn late sun
Before the weighing storm begun.

Preying, were the drones that silently honed
The rabbit infantry bounding the plain.
From bunker holes their heads were raised
As periscopes to the field,
Four-pawed troops daring the run.

Feeding, were the savages to deaths,
So cutting short of their last air-gasping breaths.

Aiming, were eagled-eyes with clasping talons,
That could carry the whole carcass slain,
The heart drowned as the murdered had died.
Hauled to the sky with such pride,
The outnumbered enemy, numb.

Bleeding from the pierced-held limped-neck,
The tender jugular forever severed.

Amazing kites to skies,
That plummet as stunt planes
To steeper-rollercoaster rise.

Their claws, venting the prize.

Then in the red-blushing set breeze,
Effortlessly they then again squadron-glide;

A pride of lions in full flight,
Hunters to innocents
That are feeders on the plains.

As the soldiers ran away,
The Air Force were plotting clever.

The Dyke slept as a stilled-lake; water dammed to a pool, fed by a river-bled stream; a long-plateaued-lock held, before it overflowed to cascade jagged rocks to where the river could then again run.

Sleepy coloured-wooden boats for rowing lay mid-water to one end, tethered, so four nosed-bows met to a centre point. Their hulls were reflected to the darkened water that stood in the shadow of the slip of woodland that run The Dyke's edge; made up of leaf-changing deciduous trees over a carpet of many-shaped leaves.

The captured water was a feeding ground to many a river bird, all living their day-to-day lives where they could beak-fish to the curling-weeded pool that was edged by taller reeds.

This all set the scene for walkers that followed the parkland side, to then parallel the woodland, aligned. The grass to the heat of the day, to then walk under trees, in the cooler shade.


**The Row Boat**


We are rowing to the river, stilled,
Blades slowly cutting the water.
The knock of oars in the row locks,
That rub as they are pushed,
Then pulled back.

The boat as a prouder peacock
Would be wearing a train, majestic;
The herring-bone trail as the boat's tail,
That plaits as it slooshes
To the near bank.

We are rowing.

The hull, angled as a bird, billed,
Gliding to ruffle the filled lake,
To wet the sides of the boat's lines,
Whooshing to silent ripple.
Quietly they span.

We are rowing.

Trees, glint-light, throwing.

Your drifting hand lifts, water-filled,
As you lean to the sides, curved.
Fingers dripping, streamlets sifting.
Tinkling, each droplet falls,
Open hand, fanned.

We are rowing.

The square blades lowing.

In the hot of day, our cares away.

Black coots call as trumpets, mute;
Dipping as divers, sea bed-fishing.

Buck ducks, quack, stood to the bank,

Swans, silent, high heads, sailing.

Our minds self-soothing,
As we're gently moving.

We are rowing ... nature's closing day.


The paddle-ducks swam in threes with walking stick crook-heads, one oblivious with a bill edge that draped river weed. They were then again dabblers to the reeds after keeping watch with a flick-turn of coloured-heads to then splay oranged-webs. A gestured quack as though a lowering musical scale echoed under the canopy of leaves, they then again sailed with rounding wakes and black and white pointing tails.

Their wider family of drakes and hens stood to the field side-edge, as though an audience to the lake show, with humoured crescendos that faded to the odd paused quack. Then a minute of silence before another would reply with laughter back. Jesters as though not a care, partying in the autumnal air.

**The Navy Drakes**

The drakes with white-chokered necks
And iridescent green-feathered heads
Laughed and laughed, as though daft,
Supporters to the swimming teams
That parallel-swam The Dyke's water still.

Wide mouths open
As gabbing friends,
Quick-gossiping bills.

Obviously thrilled.

As clowns with their brighter orange shoes,
That could topple bill-over-breast.
Drakes out, dressed to impress,
Tails groomed and head feathers greased,
The lads of the town, drunken and loud.

Swaggering-walking,
Jovially talking,
Out in the crowds.

Portside navies, proud.

The hens as plain Janes, bill-preening,
Black wigs, yellow-painted wide tight lips.
Ladies pout, standing to the bar;
Sisters wearing the same dressed-clothes,
Hoping dating sailors will take them home.

Quiet, are shying,
Dark makeup eyes,
Bills low, in hope.

The harboured-gents, without a care,
Are playing waterside inns and bars.
Hear them shout, strut out for a laugh,
A convoy of pairs eyeing the locals.
The out-of-towns, chips down, playing tables.


Along The Dyke were the everyday battles of nature, that quietly happened under the pretence of the gladed-light and unflowing water. The ducks were grouped, the coots in twos, the swans as a flotilla, whilst squirrels foraged alone. Between all these were human families and friends walking and talking; relaxed to the banks. But, if you look a little harder – amongst the trees, the leaves, nature's thieves, there sits a man alone, the woodland his home. A man who fits with nature, without life's battles, without any family or friends. Muted, he is, but would be quick to defend why he sits quiet.

**The Seated Man**

To the bank, sat, ... a solitary man.
To the thousands of leaves,
Hundreds of trees,
Tens of swans,
Squirrels, ... thick as thieves,

One man.

One ... solitary man.

A man with just one thought,
One set of clothes,
One pair of boots,
One plate, chipped curves,

And,
One ... solitary mug.

With his knees high,
Arms around, linked hands,

One ... thought-provoked man.

And,
No ... thought of a plan.

The man with one small home,
His address unknown;
One hide in woodland,
No door, one window.

One man.

One ... povertied man.

Nobody has ever reached out,
But, instead, all have looked down.

Yet,
This one man is

... An extra-ordinary man.

One, coveted man.

....

If you asked the man with no plan ...

"Do you have money, would you like money?"

He'd shy,
With nervous blink.

"Why do I need money?
 Money is deemed to pay a due."

"I have no need, I'm a man of no greed.

 I've seen the people with
 Their cars down the streets,
 Paying their bank loan debts."

"Why would I want to do that?"

....

If you asked the man with linked hands ...

"Would you like to go for a walk?"

He'd reply ...

"If you want to dance,
 You have to feel the need to dance,
 This starts with an inner beat."

"The same is to walk.
 You need something to walk to;
 To get upon your two feet.

 I have no need to walk
 As I don't know where I would go,
 Or I'd happen to find."

"Beyond the woodland are nasty surprises."

"And when I get there,
 I will have to come back."

....

You may ask the man with chin to his hand ...

"What about new clothes, or more clothes?"

He'd sigh,
With pause to think.

"I have clothes. I need no more than those."

"Every creature
 Or herd must think us as absurd.
 They only wear what they have;

 The birds with same
 Feathers, rabbits same pelt,
 The swans, laundered-white."

"To have a full wardrobe is really trite."

"Why would I want to do that?"

....

If you asked the man to the lake's banks ...

"Why do you not live in a house?"

He'd reply,
Quite matter of fact ...

"I've never owned one,
 I've never needed one!"

"Birds have nests,
 Rabbits to their burrows,
 Squirrels build their drays."

"They do not consume
 Or keep any possessions,
 They just live each day to day.

 Neither is rich, they are all stitch-poor.

 I have one window.
 I have one door.
 Why do I need more?"

....

If you dare ask the man, his words canned ...

"Why do you sit all alone?"

He'd while,
But, quickly deny ...

"I need nobody,
 I'm happy on my own."

"It starts when you're at school,
 They use classes as tools,

 You have to be one of a number.

 It continues when you work,
 They use offices for serfs.

 You then get government-fed,
 Your mind is management-led,
 Private bank account, tax-bled.

 Every person is a follower ...

Even The Pope looks to high,
The presidents, to history,

It's not only my theory ...
Why would I want to do that?"

....

"Why would you want to know that?"
Said the man, sat on his hands.

You may question, that,
If he doesn't want to walk,
And he doesn't need to talk,
He has no car, nor money,
So very few clothes –
How did he get here?

Why should you want to know?

Because,
The man with no great plans,
Who seems uncordial,
Who's deemed dull or ordinary,
Does actually, totally, utterly ...
Understand.

He is the extra-ordinary man.

For all his life, for many years long,
He played not just to society's song,

And the clothes he wears,
Although now very worn,

Are still his pride and joy;
His formal, pressed uniform.

And now, you really should know.

For the former family man,
Joined The Forces as young as he could.

His main mission,
Not his decision,

Was to find the enemy in the hills.

His battalion, four hundred, landing to shore,
In the midday sun they stood.

Boats to the rear,
With an inner fear,

Forward-marched, compassed-precision.
He, only eighteen, part of the legion.

Forward-marched,
Walking to nowhere;

Marching from rising sun.
Walking to setting skies.

His first mission,
Questioned his decision.

Uniformed in his young manhood,
Crossing borders, region to region,

Camping under Equator nights,
Hiding from the enemy's lights.

They, totally exposed;
No shade.
No trees.
No water.

Lambs to the slaughter.

Walking forth-to,
With commanded-precision.

Crossing rivers, waist-height,
Arms high, rifles in hands.

All part of the map-plotted plan ...

But torrid was the water's flow,
Horrid, as their balance, thrown.

Then shuffling to their chests,
Scuffling on elbows and legs.

Heads low, camouflaged,
... So nobody on show.

Silently, moving slow.
Beware ...
Planted mines to the grass!

He, part of the big military,
Numbered as whole solidarity.

Trekking on mountains high,
Never knowing what he'd find.

There were guerillas in the hills.

Backpacks heavy,
Onward they'd go.

Onward they'd go.

What they would find,
No maps could consider,

Even though mission-pathed,
The enemies' lines tapped,
Their signals were sapped.
Nobody was to know.
Onward they'd go.

Walking through storms of sands
That scratched their unprotected eyes,

Then land of war came in sight ...

The loudest of cannon-shot booms,
That pounded over the border lines.
Houses, as leaning cripples,
Neighbours, completely razed.

The constant blasts heard, day after day,

All over a fought-for strip of land,
As both sides constantly prayed,
Yet neither, were ever to meet.
The allies to calm open rift.

Victims maimed to naked streets.

Vehicles; cars and lorries,
Savaged and lay as crusts of war –

Once, somebody's pride and joy.

As they entered the city, torn,
Mothers cried with wailing mouths,
Their screwed, tear-bled eyes,
Such disbelief, hands held out.

Un-concerted was their manic plight.

Into heaps of concrete rubble,
Men scrambled with bare grabbing-hands,
To pull out the child that died;
Limp body, grey dust-covered.

Of hundreds at school, ... one survived.

The brass bell, still hanging to its arch,
Lain to the roadside, as a broken heart.
The sign read 'boys and girls';
Epitaph, to the day before.

The Arabic sign read 'boys and girls'!

Exhausted, with slumped shoulders,
The men dug for sons and daughters.
Ripped signs, tossed aside,
Every hand to buildings, tumbled.

Under summer weather, arid-dry,
The only rain, as every man cried.

The only rain, as *every man* cried.

The incendiaries still arced the sky.

Such disbelief, as hands held out.
The misbelief, of each religion's pride.

Just 20 years, his innocence denied.

....

Then he trained for the air corps.

Now 30, crewed flights of passion,
Flew the skies he once looked to.

The vista of pure blue.

Mountains, snow-topped.

Rivers, meandered through.

Yet,
He bombed the enemy,
Hidden to nature's glories.

If they weren't dead,
It could have been him.

Keeping eyes peeled below,

Bomb doors opened,
Away, they were blown.

But,
Little did he know.

He suddenly struck
By guerillas to the hills.

His plane, into a tail spin.

One engine caught on fire,
So spiralling out of control.

Where he crashed,
Nobody had known.

....

Now,
He captured as prisoner of war,
Bound to a chair, wrists roped.

Made to dig trenches and holes,
Build-laying long foreign roads.

All under the sun with no shade,
Made to march to their charade.

Digging to six feet below,
Digging his comrades' graves.

Their faces, unrecognised.
... Of the buried ... none were named.

Waterboarded, made to talk
The secrets of his army's war.

*One sign of stress*
*Could have been his head.*

Never to look to their eyes,
... Straight answers ... mostly were lies.

He, imprisoned,
Nobody had known.

Tortured, afraid to fall to sleep,
Torches lit the stone cell walls.

His Force's number stripped,
His bared-back strap-whipped.

Month on month,
He was on his own.

....

You could ask the man who understands ...

"Why did you go to war,
 Into a world you deplored?"

He would reply,
With reassuring eyes ...

"The outside world wasn't deplored,
 Until I went out, then came back,
 So finishing my self-exploring."

"I joined the army as a bit of a charmer."
His retort.

Then, his re-thought ...

"Because I wanted world peace;
 That the arguments,
 That the fighting,
 The caliphate battles,
 Could all be ceased."

"At such a young age,
  The Forces were my stage,
  And my country, the audience."

"But the pantomime played, became a drama."

"As our ship pulled out of port,
  To starboard side was the view,
  Where the audience,
  With the brass band playing,
  Applauded and waved."

"My part was to have the hero's heart, brave"

"But I walked so many fields,
  Hiked over mountainous-hills,
  Through deserts of too much sand.
  Forests of so many tall trees,

I realised the world was too big a place."

"As much as I tried,
  ... All heroes ... sometimes cry" ...

"But I have flown the vastest of skies,
  Seen palaces and wealth, prized.
  But, poverty; lands war-torn,
  And children with most-deadly diseases.

  ... My mission ... too big an ordeal.

  My uniform was my hero's cloak."

"Heroes only have one set of clothes."

Then, with realising eyes,
And half a twinkled smile,

"That I had more than others, dying;
  More than the hungered-babies,
  With swarming flies to eyes,
  Bandy legs and ribs like cages."

"That I did not have the millions
  Of robed-sheiks with oil fields,

  But I did have,

  A kinder heart, than the one from the start."

"And my regret,
  That, even though smart, I could've done more."

"Done more, to help the world I deplored."

"I'm still my own hero."

"Nobody may listen,
 They look from afar,
 But I've seen seven seas,
 The biggest of waves,
 Religious wars that
 Create waifen-strays.

 Held hands of the
 Families disbanded.
 Hid to save my life.

*A hint of my breath,
 Could've been my death."*

"Seen despots' slaves,
 Lived in bunkers,
 Hid in jungle trees.
 Seen a thousand graves
 Of the slaughtered ...

 Each ... with no one's name.

 Drove across tracks,
 To never look back;
 Skeletons ... rowed in lines."

....

*"There can never be world peace."*

"I've prayed at Ground Zero.

 For I haven't failed,
 Just played a part.

 Every man thinks he's a hero."

....

"The rest of my life
 Was flying against the wind,
 Battling the storm wars,
 Until I fell to a tailing-spin.

 I would then again fly,
 Defying the ground below.
 Sat in my seat, controlled,
 My colours as a skyline show.

 Little did I know.

 Again,
 The storms.

 The raging wars.

My head spinning,
With broken wings.

My engines would cut,
To then again fall.

My forward view clouded,
Aft, all that I saw ...

The women with wailing mouths,
Their square, cupped hands,

Blunt, dirt-filled, bare nails,
Their grief-chins, rounded.

The baby, dead in dust;
Black, its face,

Limp body, singed.

Momentarily,
Men cried relief.

Yet,
No words were spoken,
Tired-eyes met others,

Any console would be token.

The buildings as cripple-towers.
Trauma, so target-planned.

Templed-domes –
Now bare bones.

Discarded shoes to the ruins.

My mind has lied
In its own grave ...

With no coffin,
Six feet under."

"The same ... as those men with no names."

....

"I hold the medal for helping
The world I deplored.

But now *my* mind needs its help,
By that world, I'm ignored."

....

If you asked the man,
Seemingly always sad ...

"Why is this your life?"

He'd reply,
With a reflective mind ...

"I cannot forget the
 Wailing mouths;
 Utter, exceptional grief ...

 As the enemy smiled, proud."

"It is easier to be at one,
 With continual sadness ...

 Than have love,

 Have family,

 Have possessions,

 The momentary glory you bought,
 Love-minutes to the mind, stored,

 ... Bad continual thoughts,

 Than lose love,
 Lose family,
 And become a lesser ...

 Through heartache or contempt,
 And have a mind of resentment."

"So, if
 I never love,

 Or never know,

 And never have,

 With nothing to worry about,
 I can think more clearly,

 It's not only my theory ...

 Why would I want to become that?"

 ....

"My whole heart as a hero,

 Just one possession;
 One badge of honour.

My soul, seeing the rear view."

....

The red kites in the skies,
Remained as cross planes.

The swans their own armada,
As though on their guard.

The coots, as quick-shoots;
Divers hunting survivors.

Trout, so still whilst feeding,
Dull submarines to weeds.

The squirrels as mine planters,
Then to scurry to trees,
In a hurry, high lookout spies.

And to the camouflage of leaves,

One solitary man.
One set of clothes.

# White Man's Land of Freedom

**Rock-A-By**

In the glimpse of moonlight.
The early hours of the morn,

One woman to the shelter-porch,
Singing to the sleeping child;
It held in her mothering-arms.

Singing soft lullabies,
Until baby ... no longer cries.

One women to her rocking chair,
Whisp'ring to the hours, tired.
Blanketing with covering-arms.

Singing soft hush-a-bies,
To the back-choir of the owl hoot-night.

One woman in the cross bar light ...

Where the moon slinks through
The torched-railings in lines,

... Listening to the crickets' choir,

Lullaby,
Hush-a-by night.

Rocking baby,
To the creek of the chair;
Its tempo
The rhythm of dreams,

As the moths' wings
Douse-flicker candled-light,

Lullaby.
Rock-a-by night.

To and fro
To sleep he'll go.

With a peep through drawn, watery-eyes
At the rounded wolf-moon's glow,

Off to sleep he'll go.

Lullaby.

To and fro,

The creeking, oh so slow.

The frogs chirrup to the dawn.

Back and forth,
To and fro.
Lullaby,

To your dreams do go.

The cool of nighttime air,
After the hot, tinder-dry day,
Where tumbleweed blew,
The outback, through.

When the heat of the sun
Made a parched-throat, baked,
No oasis be seen
To the mirage sheen.

Shhhhh ...
Lullaby.
Rock-a-by night,

Twinkle stars bright in
Hush-a-by sky.

To and fro,

The creeking, oh so slow.

Back and forth,
To and fro.

Storms of last season,
Far behind, hatches latched
against the rain,
Now, again, stay open.

Farmers scythed the summer grain.

Shhhhh ...
Rock-a-by.
Lullaby sung to sleepy eyes,
Pass the night of creeping dreams.

....

But in the quiet of night
The world doesn't seem right ...

There is a shroud of cloud
Wanting the moon's position.

For the mother, her love shared,
To the horizon, stares.

In the reflected glint,
There are tears to her eyes.

Listen.

Lullaby.
Lullaby, low.

For the women, to creeking chair,
Holds consolation in her arms.

With no clothes, babe lies bare,
And she, just a rag to her back.

Mumbling.
Lullaby.
Hush-a-by, slow,

The bats' wings as the fright show.

"White man came from dem hills,
 White man on horses' backs;
 Galloping fast,
 Shout'n' 'n' screamin',
 Wakin' the village from their beds.

 White man came in dark of night,
 Lit-torches, fire in hands
 As guidin' masts,
 Hollerin' 'n' screamin'
 Settin' light to dem wood'n shacks."

"Dem houses, our homes."

"Flames of fury, as the jury,
 Made us sin-guilty for not givin' in."

"Sheriff didn't have no writ.
 Our men with long poles to fight.
 White men wore masks,
 Stood strong to the village,
 Savages raped our community life."

"Bastards raped some black men's wives."

....

Crumbling.
Lips tight.
Round eyes gaped,
Tear-wells of fright.

"Dem mens our husbands."

"Beat'n to never come back."

"Allah, I pray they don't die."

White man with torches
Reflected in her eyes ...

The creeking slow,
To and fro ...

Lullaby,
Let your grief cry.


**The Ship**

Billowed-sails, to the ocean waves,
Aiming for the working fields.

Riddled slaves, to the boat's dark hold,
The black men sweating to the bilge.

Timbers creeking,
As it lows,

Not knowing where they're going.

Not seeing what lies ahead,
Still, envisage their village stead.

Lullaby,
To and fro,

Sleep-hunched as
The main stow.

Dem ladies, their wives,
They're left behind.

All alone.

Lullaby,
To and fro.

Big men,
Hands to heads,
Covering eyes,
Let your grief cry.

No water, no food,
Some are the dead.

Sleep to the creeks.
Let dead men lie.

If not thrown overboard,
They be buried the other side.

To and fro,
Dip to the flow.

Hearts sinking,
White men to thinking.

Dem wives
There for pillage and rape.

The men holding own-faith.

To and fro,
None o' them will know.


**The Wood'n Church**

"The Lord, our saviour,
 He is my brave,
 Looking over us
 Every day."

The preacher with hands,
Open, holding the air,

Head to low, Sunday mornin'
Calling the Baptists' prayers.

"The Lord, is amongst us,
 He is our stave,
 Looking after your
 Families, back there."

"Sing to the Lord!"

The sayer, smile so wide,
How can he be denied.

And so the men sang,
Hoping for console it brang.

They sang and sang.

But the angst took its toll.

They sang and sang,

Yet in the air of the wooden church,
There was something The Lord couldn't touch.

The organist,
Played and played,

Conviction hands to the keys,
Heavy and loud ...

So the crying was drowned.

The sayer to crowd
Prayed and prayed,

Lifted his voice so very much,
There was denial to his reprisal.

The singing, to an odd word lowed,
The Lord didn't shift the black gents' woes.

Cry, man, cry,
Let your grief go.


**The Slaves**

We are the thought-of poor,
Those, never thought as more.

Chain-slaved to rich man, white,
Field workers to the master's estate.

Renamed for the boss's list.

Quiet
Singing whilst cotton pickin'.
With baskets to our backs,
We are the little-taught more.

Low tone,
Hummin' while loadin' the ships,
With boxes to our hands.
We are the bought-for core.

High five,
Whistlin' slow through fields of beet.
With scythes to the lands,
We, part of the black-trade law.

Brought to the promise land;
The land of white men's cause.

Whilst we're singing,
The Mas'er's bank's ringing.

Our names as easy to speak.

....

We have looked to the eagled-sky,
They have freedom of flight.

We have tickled fishes to the stream,
They swim and swim as free.

Ickle are their lives,
Yet they are survivors.

....

Polite,
Singing whilst fruit plant pickin',

Hummin', loading teak clippers,
Whistlin', carrying the sheathed-wheat.

The Mas'ers don't know what we're thinking.

We be praying for the air-flown dream,

Far beyond the plantation house flag,
That boasts about the capture of man.

Far beyond the mansion's gate.


In January 1863 Abraham Lincoln's emancipation proclamation of black-slaved folk began, giving freedom from the ties of the white men of the U.S. – his part of the abolition of slavery.

The black folk now had hope. They had jobs to now be employed, so what more could they need?

Hope.


**The Freedom Walk**

'Ccordin' to Congress law
We ain't to be slaved no more.

Smiling,
Whilst we plan our own homes,

Laughing,
As we pick up our bags,
Walking together,
Talking of freedom.

We're walking back home.
Home, to where we belong.

Walking the Sugar Beet Road,
The cane, no longer our load.

So many years, we've b'n wronged.

This is *our* land of freedom,

Yet,
We walk as black men, branded;
With stars to our arms,
Scars to our hearts
And
Stripes across our backs.

We are.
We are.
We are,

The men of hands from the land.

Freed from the fists of slavery,
To triumphant clenches of bravery.

We are,

Singing loud, as the proud.
Our bags packed to our backs.

Walking from the portside boats,
The ships, no longer free-stowed.

We are.

....

We are,

Peoples with the heart of dem eagles,
We have made real, the dream of them.

Our hope became reality,
We now have the flight of freedom.

....

And to the country
We built our own shacks.

We knows these are our homes.

And sittin' to the to and fro,
Us free men ...

Crickets sing to the thicket,

Twinkle stars bright in
Hush-a-by sky,
Homeland moon beams so bright

... With wives, in reflective thoughts.

Humming, whilst guitar-strumming.

Singing our native lullabies.

And in the silenced-dark,
Our night ears hark ...

Mmmm, mmmm,

Creeking rockers to shelter-porches.

# The Seated Man 2

"Wake up."
A voice said with demand.

"I rolled over, bleary-eyed,
  He stood to the other side."

"Get up."
His wanting, an instant.

"I tried to orient my head,
  Where was I, ... lying in bed?"

"Up, now."
He had great insistence.

"With water over my eyes,
  Where I hadn't slept all night.

I dreamt metal doors clanging,
  The jangle of keys, turning locks.

Then, light through the door,
  The dark night without a clock.

The room oozed such cold,
Light glimpsed angular corners,
No window,
A single shade,
That hung over where I laid."

"Get up!"

"My single blanket sheet,
  Pulled off from head to feet.

I slowly rose, steady to go,
On the edge of its ledge,
Rigid hands wiped tired eyes."

"Come!"

"He took hold of my arm,
  Ready to walk the floor.

I pulled away from my elbow
To resist as insolence.
My head looked down, so tired and worn."

"COME!"

"I stood and followed,
  Every word, to bare room, echoed.

Corridors.

Corridors long, cold,
Without any light.

Guided by my arm,
My hands rear-cuffed,

Chained as a slave.
Shackles to my ankles.

Two men, foreign voices.
Without looking, both unshaven,
Swarthy-skinned,
The smell to breaths
Told they'd been smoking.

Hallways, subdued,
Without end in sight.

Not a single window,
In concrete high walls.

Two men, military boots,
I glimpsed, while looking down;
Heavy leather,
Hardly cleaned,
Ricocheted was the pounding.

The basement's coldness,
Tingled my nose hairs.

My ears detecting,
Every minute, distant sound.

I heard others shouting,
Beating doors, wanting attention.

Heard prisoners calling,
Kicking walls, with frustration.

Doors after doors,
Cells after cells,
Each with bars
Over tiny glass."

....

He, the prisoner of war,
His mind picking earlier years.

Replaying the fear.

Scared beyond scared,

That that was life's end.

**The Man Who Held The Sky**

Out there, outside your window, your door, are people who do not want to be ignored; people who find a reason, not necessarily rhyming or chiming with others, some dependent on humanity's cyclical emotionally-invested, irrational seasons. Integrally, their own self-hero. Each has focused on one thing to be their aim, and in doing so, they self-proclaim their goodness without modesty. Honestly!

The minorities have more to say than the majorities, and is they who try to sway every passing child, woman and man to walk the same way; the 'righteous' path of *their* mind. Some, crowd-funding sympathy, empathy or anything as gain.

See them stand to boxes on corners, sit in the trees or proclaim from any higher place where others can see them.

Outside the town, overlooking down, is a high grassed-mound named Speakers' Hill. It is almost biblical, where past prophets have preached in their robes to the listening-crowds. The long tradition has been centuries-kept with regular sayers and the annual bell-ringing mayor all having their say. One can imagine on sunshine days the town's folk could walk up and debate with the talkers. By building a community they could build immunity to the controversial world they purveyed.

Atop is the Centennial Rock that is perched to the hill's peak; a monument to thinkers, where smaller stones have become paperweights for people's written-notes of thought and opinion.

Stand, speak out, beyond your doubt and gather others to your fold. But there is another story to be told ...


**Speakers' Hill**

With buttoned-mouth she ran with fury,
Ran to the peak of the hill.
Nobody could stop her,
Nobody would want to.

And If she stood before judge and jury,
She would be charged as guilty
For shouting profanities
To the whole of humanity.

For her caged-tongue she bears,
Is the wild of her mind,
That when unleashed
Breaks the township's serene.

For she needs a clear blue mind,
And if bad days get in the way,
Where life's skies become opaque,
Fellow man is no longer kind,

She has to let it all out.

....

Others were happy in their way,
Patiently waiting the change of weather.

....

With zipped-lips she ran with fury,
Fast-ran up Speakers' Hill.

Nobody should stop her.

Bursting her fastened-mouth,
Her head forward, stretched neck,
And eyes, large-bulging,

She curses regular Tourette's.

For she screams and screams,
To the imperfect weather,
Until the clouds pass away.

Hurls and hurls abuse
When the sky brings her down,
She blusters as its counter.

The weight stones are thrown
To the cumulus above her,
Falling on men and the church.

Listening to the Sunday choir
That ambles through streets,
Overwhelming are her expletives.

....

And the written-opinions
Posted to the great rock,
Are there to feel her rage.

For
The Woman Who Shouts at Clouds,
With her hands over ears,
Outing what her mind holds,
Raging clout to the world,

Has lost all her self-control,

As the Speakers' Hill's troll.

....

If you asked the woman
Who attacks the crowds,

"Why are you shouting?"

She would say that it's a bad day,
The clouds are in the sun's way.

"How can I have the day spending,
 With heavy weather impending?
 And clouds lead to rain,
 That then become storms."

....

She's been seen with her bristle broom,
At the top of Mount Speakers',
With it stretched up high,
Two gripped-hands, constantly air-beating.

Slamming and slamming,
The blowing storm's air-damning.

But with her angst and her fury,
They still won't go away.
Stood higher to Listeners' Seat,
Still she is raging and raging.

....

If you asked Ms. Tourette's,
Who's blazing has little affect ...

"Why do you not calm down?"

She would frown as scorn,
A look to belittle your question.

She will tell ...

"This is Speakers' Hill and
 It can be any one's will
 To proclaim their thoughts;
 Unto others they be taught,
 And so the day becomes better."

But ... only better in *her* mind.

For she is the scourge of the church,
To the town's folk, witch-hissing,
To every woman, the troubling bitch,

Yet,
She cannot see that it's not the sky at fault,
She is just making it her self-reasoning,

As
No man, no woman, no church,
Upon paper, through spoken word
Can contra her blinkered-opinion.

Their life beliefs, besmirched.

Her harsh words are of concern,
And even democracy cannot move her.

She will tell that

The Right of Speech,
As the church's to preach,
And men shouldn't be allowed,
And women should just keep home,
Children to sit quiet, not talking.

She is the making of everyone's day,
... And the breaking for what they prayed.


**The Man In The Tree**

The cameras, all focused high.
Each man adjusting his lens
To get the best picture they can.

Heads peering up, one eye shut,
The shutter to make the news.

The man who is sitting in the tree,
Says that he represents you and me.

"Why are you up there?" They ask.
"When are you coming down?"
"He can't stay there forever!" They muse.

The man who is sitting in the tree,
Is staying,
To come down, he is refusing!

The bulldozers are waiting;
Waiting to flatten the land
Where the tree will no longer be ...

The tree that was here
Before you, me and he.

The prime minister, who is
Now seen as sinister,
Wants a bypass to trespass,
To allow thousands of cars
As though doing the conga,
To dance in their long lines
As though a vehicle spine,
Lining the edge of the town.

Half of the residents are frowning,
Yet, they'll drive cars to use the pass.

Half of the locals are smile-cheering;
Cheering, lorries won't fill small streets.

The man who is sitting in the tree,
Is saving;
Saving nature, not coming down.

The journalists still stare,
Asking questions;
Inane queries to fill pages.

Locals are now arguing the cause,
Because everyone has their opinion.

The man who is sitting in the tree,
Is debating:
More pollution is not the solution.

The clown Mayor who is
Claiming to be vocally-clever,
Says that fewer lorries in town
Will bring death rates down;
People will live much longer.
Local jobs created,
It's been much debated,
He will allow cafés on streets.

The shop owners berate on their own,
Alone, as they will lose needed-trade;

Trade that came from the many pass-throughs
Who stop to shop, their town, they are using.

The man who is sitting in the tree,
Is smiling;
Smiling, he has created such anarchy.

Police coercing him down,
Shout out the law,
He is not helping himself.

The road builders are charging;
Charging the government –
For all the wasted wait-time.

....

After 6 months,
The man in the tree finished his stunt.

After 2 years,
The residents were full of such cheer …

A beautiful spine road,
That took off the load,
So the town is quiet.
This, instead of arguing,
People speak on the street.
More are now stopping
To do weekly-shopping.

Yet every person had an opinion.
They debated, each much-remonstrated.

Some fell out, without a doubt,
Now together they all laugh;

Happy consumerists, shopping,
Car back seat, school kid-dropping.
With longer journeys,
Much more they are earning.

And,
The government's taking more taxes.

The road to be the PM's legacy,
Yet, he'll never be remembered,
Nor the tree, fatally-dismembered,

But,
Only, ... the man who *sat* in the tree;

The man who played democracy.
Who stopped the government scheming,
Stopped the Mayor from deeming,
Put his own town in the papers,
Made the residents look at their lives.

And,
Showed that democracy is hypocrisy.

There will never be skylarks
Over the tree-flattened park,

That is now tarmac-laden.

....

Yet one journalist reported,
From the mayhem, retorted ...

"So, why did it take so long,
 For the man in the tree
 To come down for a pee,
 And have a much-needed bath?"

## Sugar Loaf Hill

Is he the new Messiah?

There, higher than high,
He thinks, crossed-legged on his own,
And sits in a hollowed-tree,
Far beyond where we can climb,
On nigh, to Sugar Loaf Hill.

No life yields on the rocky crop,
Yet,
The skeleton tree has always been.

The shadowed-man is rarely seen,
Yet,
As the sun rises, he prays.
As the sun sets, he stands
Arms wide
As though a figured-cross.

His hands, commanding the night;
A conductor to the stars, the moon,
And the colours of auraed-lights.
A magician with his wand,
He is far beyond, either you or I.

Is he the son of a god?

He stands above the crowd that bays.
He has been much written about,
Yet,
Nobody knows his name.

Theologians have looked
At biblical dates,
Believing two thousand years.

A hope been forever conceived.

Pinpointing the past days,
He must be Heaven's brother.
There are no proclaimed-others.

....

They had heard of mighty Titans
Who held up pillars, astride,
Those as tall as mountains,
And, some ever-suffering,
Holding the world as a boulder.

....

Nobody can visit the rocky crop,
So, how did he get there?

He's a man so revered,
With hands that are demanding,
Yet he seemingly so at peace,

He has one shoulder-dove as his love.

Not that anybody really knows,
But, how does he exist?
Still the journalists persist.

....

Over years, great rains did fall,
The clouds rolled over more and more,
Floods broke the rivers' banks,
Super-hot months became a norm.

Still, he commanded the weather.

Each evening his hands felt the air,
Through the darkened-nights,
Silhouetted 'fore lightning strikes.

But
Mostly, sat in the solitary, hollow tree.

....

He sent the white messenger dove,
To fly over the humaned-Earth,
Over the commercialed-world,
To return back to Sugar Loaf
With dark feathers from polluting smoke.

....

The followers wrote proclamation.
Most dismissed him not wise,
Not everyone needed 'The Messiah';
The freak on the hill, mentally-ill.

The weather was hand-held,
Each year-change was heart-felt.

For he sent the herd a warning,
Their sin was the global warming.
No longer could he hold the skies,
No more could the gods be quelled.

Prepare for a world of hell.

....

Then came the thundered-night;
The Great Storm, mid-July.
Much noise of angered-gods,
The lightning cast at angles.
Such rage of the rain,
Savaging to flooded plains.

Disciples with drenched clothes
Stood to the base of the hill,
With torn, ravaged hair,
Rain pelting their faces,
Hoping he could tame the storm.

The tree to the hill was lurching,
A raven perched to its only branch,
Cawing to the flashes, frightening.
Was this Hell's final message?
Was this the end of the world?

....

Then,
In the morning, the rock calm,
One woman looked up
To exclaim the disappeared-tree.

Where was the man of Sugar Loaf?
The man who ruled the climes.

Every night, no hands beared,
Every morn, no knelt-prayers.

In the coloured rising sun
The hill stood as naked, bare.

....

Through years, some whispered,
Others, couldn't have cared,

For
The man, with his finger wands,
Played nothing to their lives.

But more the floods flooded,
So more the rains gained,
Much more the oceans rose,

More, the disciples wrote
Of The Man ... Who Held The Sky.
The brother who held the heavens.

He was the coming-Messiah,
Who warned the world of greed,
Warned man of the greater need,

But didn't speak, didn't preach,
As,
All mankind has muffled-ears.

Their chance, once again missed.
Will he come back in two thousand years?

... Maybe,
Only if Mother Earth still exists.


**The Field Feeders**

"We are saving animals and the world!"

The flocking sheep have more colour than they,
Together to the field, eating greenery and hay.
As beyond the town's slaughterhouse;
The sacrificial church of meat-eaters,
Are the couple who prefer God's land.

Not content with their thought to eat,
Together they almost bleat as they preach.

See them sitting to the hedge,
Eating nature's fruits hanging,
Snuffling foliage of anything rooted,
And milk from grown nut and husk.

Others wipe blood off their plate,
This couple moo as though cud-chewing.

They would be happier on all fours,
And even though Jesus served fishes
To please the hungried-crowd,
They are happy eating plain bread.

See them supermarket hoarding,
Fake meat-tasting food for their disorder.

Even though they're self-boasting,
Righteous, carrot-munching hosts,
They never seem happy, a smile of wry,
They've never laughed, for want of trying.

Even though they share the same fields,
Some are still not friends to the sheep,
To the beef, or the fat-porking pigs,
As they rate them as methaned-polluters.

The plated-hog-wolfing gents
Are giving them long breadth,
Yet the restaurants serve their food
At high prices, for what is so crude.

Ask them their cause, they will pause ...

"We're saving lives."

"Non-exploitation of animals,
 To save the world, to stop
 Greenhouse gases, methane-
 Producers in their masses,
 To be happy, to be slimmer."

Then tell them what becomes their cause –

Synthetic garments mass-produced
With slave and child labour,
That burn fossil fuels,
Nothing can be recycled,

Their veg and ideas grown in manure.

"We're being ethical."

Yet,
They drive cars on deadly-oil,
Clogging their cities,
Shortening all lives,
Flying high on holiday planes,
Their food flown from far islands.

And those do-gooding electric cars,
Lithium-batteried,
Phones and devices,
Killing the fishes to the rivers;
Exploiting, what they're supporting.

The omnis keep heads low,
Pointing out The Queen has beefeaters.

The couple feel ignored,
What could they do next?

To stand their ground, they come off field,
To climb to the top of Free Choice Hill,
And wearing fake fleeces to backs,
Jaw-chewing, they ruminate as show ewes;

As slope animals, so all can see them.

So everyone look at the fad of the season,
Stay to your plates, or grass feed as these vegans.

# The Seated Man 3

"What is your name?"

"I am a soldier of Her Majesty's army."
He replied direct and loud.
Eyes straight to the wall,
Almost looking through them.

"What is your name?"

"I am captain 45563219."

"YOUR NAME!"

Both were smoking,
One with cigarette in fingers,
The other hanging half from lips.

They looked at each other.

A third had finger to trigger.

The room dark, echoed their words,
The shouts rebounding the walls.
One small table,
Three chairs,
One cabled-bulb,
One frame to the wall;

He was their leader,
Medals to chest,
Eyebrows so dark,
His eyes stared to him.

Each rebel soldier gave salute.

....

His mind's ordeal, still felt real.

He, their pride-hostage was retribute.

The men in boots were there to kill.

# Upon Speakers' Hill

Ms. Tourette's is shouting;
Shouting about non-meat eaters,
Vowing to tempt them with bacon –
The smell, unmistaking.
Served between two slices,
With butter, with sauce.

They can't live without sausage!
Scowling about lard-fat bangers,
Snout-snuffling pigs heads' mix,
The spit, air-taking.
Salt-preserved and protein,
To fatten her cause.

Shouting and shouting,
But never self-doubting.

However, she's inviting;
Inviting the journalist to write,
Why grass-feeders are wrong.

The cameras are pointing;
Pointing to the fake sheep –
Hill-grass-eating,
To make their main feature.

Her rant, over-portioned,
Vowing their smug demeanour
Allows her some mickey-taking,
The fields manured;
Their crops forced.

Denouncing, denouncing,
A spell to renounce them.

She's very inciting;
Inciteful to those not taking note,
And vote-makers are weak.

The weather over the vegans' meal,
Is storming for the rest of the week.

## The Lives of Women

## The Eternal Beach

To the wind-driven golden sands
They sat with a blanketed-picnic for two.
Chequered was the patterned-rug
That cushioned them as props to the groyne.

She, beautiful with dress to impress,
Woven straw hat brim-shading her eyes.
He, so handsome with sleeves rolled
High, and hemmed-shorts curving his knees.

Alone to the middle of the beach,
Stood, admiring the summer day
The teen second-glanced the couple,
Romancing, smiles and glasses.

The lady quick-shivered a chill,
The gent offered his arm as comfort.

Oh, how chivalry was not dead,
Envy to her mind encumbered.

....

She saw herself, again, as a young
Virgin to the eternal beach,

When she wanted to have love,
Kiss love with embraced passion.

So fair, but an age to breach
The boundaries of her girlhood.

How innocent was her mind
That her first love would be forever.

Alone to the middle of the beach,
The moment, thought to a stare.

Her blond long hair breeze-brushed.
The flavour of love, she savoured.

....

Now
She is walking the eternal beach,
Every day she rakes the sands.
She rakes and rakes,
To give order to her mind.

She can keep walking forward
Along the beach of her life,
To the end, the sunset lies.

But she prefers to stroll back,
Along the length of the reach,
When she, younger, as the sun rose.

Each day she rakes the ruffled sand,
Parallel in lines between groynes,
The waves lapping her life's time.

Not happy walking forward,
She's analysing each part with strife.

Analysing beyond analysing,
The anxiety, paralysing.

Each footstep back-traced,
Counting each of the grains.

She is searching for her lost treasure,
That once, could pleasure her days.

Then, disbanded as not needed,
It was chucked to the sea;
Thrown beyond her memory beach.

The weathered groynes mark years;
Between each, the time she had.
Ahead could be shells of pearls,
Could be the lucky buried trove;
Sunnier days to gable-painted huts.

Analysing beyond analysing,
The anxiety, paralysing.

Her onward mind's door, forever shut.

....

Shake the woman of the beach,
Her reaching eyes can't see the sky,
That is spanning bluer going forward,

Preferring the grey clouds behind,
Where sometimes the sun glimpsed,
Each pinch-held as proud memories.

Her pure thoughts, now, much tainted.

....

If you asked the woman
With tines to the sand ...

"What are you doing, day after day?"

She will tell you
She has lost a key;
Dropping it, momentarily.

When actually, she has lost her way.

But, dig a little deeper,
The key's clumsy keeper,
Isn't truth-telling
By the sea's swelling.

She has lost the key to her heart.

For
She held a lock as her guard,
The key plopped to the sand
In hope that her steeded-knight
Would pick her upon his saddle
And canter the eternal beach;
Onward to ever-blue skies
Forward to the sun to set;

Onward through lapping tides.

For sake of sakes,
Her pretences faked,

In the surf's drawing wake.

....

She can see herself young of heart,
Seeing the lovers to the middle groyne.

The gent, fore-fronting her dreams.

Having seen others to the water's edge,
She has walked in hand, within her mind.

Yet, the man of men she'd never find.

She has kissed,
She has hugged,
Swooned to love's tune.

But the gent of gents to the dunes
Would never become her life-real.

Raking and raking,
It's so heart-breaking,

....

If you asked the woman,
Her mind gold-panning ...

"Why are you re-treading your footsteps?"

She will spellbind
That history is good,
And helps your way forward.

When actually, her foresight is inept.

But, pretence enlightened,
Her eyes are a lot darker,
Her tremble-lips brave
In the crash of the waves.

No love, has her heart ever swept.

Raking and raking,
Quick-shake her,
A better life, forsaking.

....

Her mind damning beyond damning,
She's within her life's drama.

The gent to the sun-drenched divide,
Would and could never provide.

She can dream of marriage for two,
But her horse to carriage, would never them pull.

For,
No man could take the gent's
Place, to walk hand in hand.
The combination to her inner
Was just his for the turning.
She only yearned his smile,
His touch, as mind-spangled.
A kiss to offered chisel lips,
That could keep a sunnier day.

Her footsteps meander the sand,
Then she rakes them as never there.

Raking and raking,
Swift-hand,
Smoothing her heartbreak,

To her breast ... you can see her breath race.

....

If you asked the woman
What are her plans ...

She will tell you,
"This is my happy place."

Convincing, smiling, her face.

When actually, her character's deadpan.

With the sunlight behind,
You can actually see through her ...

See the wisp of sand to the wind
That swirls and swirls her being.
The seagulls circle her skyline,
Her mind-kite torn to the storm.
The love that she so wanted,
Squandered, through growing years.
Her ice cream days now melted,
With no sandprints to the horizon.

At 50, she is looking at her life.
There was no park stroller
To the beach waves that rolled,
No tiny hands held to fizzle sea
Where childhood kicking begins.
No shoulder holds of son on dad,
Or the teenager becoming a man.

Some of her friends are already dead.

The eternal beach shows plight as a whole,
The spined-groynes of time, weathered.

The fair maiden, a virgin, salt-cured.

She rakes and rakes a mind, disordered,

But, ... that heart-breaking life ... has no soul.

## The Window Cleaner

Mid-autumn, grey were the clouds,
As she cleaned cloth to window.

Late morning, round and around,
As she soaped glass and frames.

And she soaped and soaped,
Then she wiped and wiped,

Yet, ... no clearer was her view.

And she wiped and wiped,
Then did polish and polish,

Yet, no clearer the view, through.

....

That, the day of his funeral.

Each Tuesday she cleaned and cleaned,
Remembered respect to he,
Their home still had to gleam.

....

In the light of the glass,
She saw their years, past:

Her veiled-face to marriage vows,
He lifted for the confirmed kiss.

The curtains long he pulled open,
Just before they made passionate love.

The car's door he offered to,
Such a gent who had respected her.

... In blue stiletto heels,
And bent two knees,
Swivelled to sit in tight skirt.

So, her eyes welled a blur.

And she soaped and soaped,
Then she wiped and wiped,

Still, no clarity to her view.

Mid-autumn, grey were the clouds,
As she cleaned cloth to window.

....

Through the looking-glass pane,
His life-end became borne bane:

His paled-glaze to hospital bed,
The listless hand that could never hold,

Privacy curtains pulled closed,
The moment, she kept the world out.

... She knelt to the bed,
As though her last prayer,
To kiss his sleeping forehead.

Her mind casting love over doubt.

And she wiped and wiped,
To the glass panes as dry,

Sunlight, inched to her view.

October, the forlorned clouds,
As she finished to thinking.

The pause to clarity,
Checking the edges,
Inspecting frames.

She threw the cloth to the floor.
In the moment of her upset

She could take little more,

She dropped to all fours.

The cloth grabbed to her grip,
She sobbed her heart through.

The cotton corner to eyes,
She cried beyond crying.

Sobbed beyond sobbing,
Her whole life robbed.

This the day of his funeral,
The final relief of him dying.

From disbelief, to the future, saw.

The glass had needn't been cleaned,
As she had wiped it ... every day before.

....

She remembered his last breath,
The words, "I love you" lying his death bed.

## The Hill of Pills

Her mind always has pending bad weather,
So, at five to nine she queues the queue for one,

She will look to the left, look to the right,
Back over her shoulder; look behind.

Handbag in clutched hands,
She will open the clasp
And check through tissues,
Cigarettes and matches,
In case she forgot she still had tablets.

Her fingers are shuffling;
Shuffling to the left, shuffling right,
To the bottom, then she'll look behind.

Tiniest strap watch to wrist,
Her two fingers pinch
To check the precise time;
Minutes to seconds,
Over her low-nosed bone-rimmed glasses.

Could she have a headache from looming weather?

Her mind will always have one cloud of gloom,
And it's never too soon for another pill.


Door sign turning, is concerned
And scuffles a little forward.
Looking left, quick right and then behind.

Blue handbag in tightest grip,
The clasp twisted closed,
Palm to head, feigning her pains.

For The Lady Who Is Always Ill

Never thinks any different,
Will always predict ahead
Instead of living the moment.

Checking time, looking left,
Looking right, the bottom of her bag,
To then look behind.

Her life lived by hoarding little boxes,
Some think it quite odd.
Cigarettes, matches and tablets,
To get her through her storm.

The blue sky days never seem
To be breaking her bad weather.

She will never get to the top
Of her hill ... built of tablet box-pills,

With each, hoping to get a bit higher,

Yet,
She'll always go around her mountain's middle.

Holding tight, small steps,
Looking down, hardly up,
To the right, the left, always behind.

To never have a rainbow in her sight.

If she reached her peak
She could look lower to know ... that she was never ill.

## The Seated Man 4

"I can't forget the women with wailing mouths."

"Sheer devastation, forts between nations."

"Sad flags that boundaried both sides,
 Hung limp to no wind, against warring skies.

 Even their crowns' colours were down."

....

"Every Quran wrote eye for an eye,
 That became head for a head,
 Child for a child.

 Over centuries the words were re-read,
 Over millennia, became 'mega-death upon death'.

 Each cried for their loved ones dying,
 Yet the cause was never more plausible,

 That made any agreement impossible."

"The grief of one can never be undone.
 The grief of a hundred holds a cause,
 And a thousand makes the unhappiest of wars."

"No victory flag should ever fly
 To the destruction of other men's lives."

*"There will never be religious peace."*

....

"Bad heart will pump black
 Blood through veins of regions."

"Dark minds will psyche
 New findings of far told-people."

"Few guns control
 The lives of the many ..."

"Tracked-tanks will flatten
 Seized peace towns ... of plenty."

....

"The bombs may be signed by their idols,
 Designed for temple destruction,
 Their gold shells show the way to Hell."


....


"No thrush sung to the dawn of dust.
 The sun's ball of fire challenged the day
 As imams haled ... and both sides prayed."


....


"Why would I want to go for a walk?

 The town's folk debate and talk,
 Some are repeating and repeating
 On the hill of Mount Speakers'.
 I can see the start of a riot.
 It's getting beyond a game."

"The people happy going around and around,
 Never getting to agree a single cause."

"Around and around ... until their eyes are drawn."

"The Mayor is calculating his load,
 Priority is sought with picked-short straws."


....


Surrounding The Dyke
Black birds are loud morning-crowing,
Coloured ducks vocal and proud,
Pied magpies are rattling,
The swans glide
Self-musingly quiet.
And
Circling kites are stretched-wide-to-skies,
Catching freshest wind-to-wing.

Nature was together singing.


....


"No thrush sung to the dawn of dust."


.

## The Centennial Rock

The notes under stones
Are becoming excessive;
Each opinion is self-plausing,
Not helping the town's causes.

Words slammed in capitals,
Punctuation expressive,

And the hill speakers are now grouping;
Cliques with a common bond,
And those beyond are the enemy.

The journalists are filling papers;
Filling columns about protesters.

They are the making of town's clouds;
Marking two sides to the streets,
With pass-throughs down the middle.

The shopkeepers are stocking;
Stocking gossip at counters.

Sympathetically nodding,
They are boxing clever.

Spires bell-ring in the east,
The towers peel to the west,

Fliers are handed around.

Whilst the Mayor is brass-clanging,
To hold the crowd's every man's ground.

Those barking, wanting him disrobed,
Are quietly fed the juicy charity bone.

....

There is no respected flying flag
Who's past is tied to a saluted-mast.

**La Bête Noire**

Relaxed was the melodic piano that paused on the final chord, to continue as reverberation under the polite appreciation fingertip clapping, waving through the dark of the bar, to the last of singled-applause. Some still cosied their glasses in hands to realise that through the piano man's last playing session there was just a sip left for lips. Eyes were averting to search the attention of white shirt waiting staff that meandered the tables.

The odd ceiling lamp glinted the edge of silver trays held high above heads of seated-guests, each circled the tall and stemmed glasses with centred cubed-ice buckets. The waiters still taking requests after a click of fingers while passing, or giving the cigared-men a match light.

### 1. The Bar

Glasses clinked in the fingers of the waiter,

Copper shades lowered to the bar.

The silhouetted-gentlemen hold whiskey on ice,

A cigarette held idling in fingers,

The glowing smoke waves in its rise.


Jazz piano tinkles in a darkened corner,
The script sheets thumbed through its play.
The low voice, walnut eyes, Africaan his skin,
Wooden slats to the window highlight
The open lid with parallel lines.

Portraits in black and white hang across the wall;
Generations of players, past.
The direct eyes, soften' hue and whiter smiles,
Each one, its own hanging brass light,
Along side concert promotion signs.

People talk in triangular light.

Waiters hold drinks on trays held high.

Ladies schmooze with their smiles bright,

Gentlemen relax, crossed-legged, crossed wrists,
Ashtrays to side.


The bar was not just a jazz 'n' drink den, it also sold love 'n' drugs. Even though it was a lounge house in the upmarket side of the town of gangsters, it would serve to all: the ladies of societied-perfumes, the trend-setting rich gents and the sailors off portside.

Serve to all, so long as they were white.

## 2. The Classy Lady

Across well-trodden boards she walked high in heels,
Tall legs in black shorter skirt,
Loose-necked white cotton revealed her chest,
A diamond cross in the vee of her shirt.

With forefinger and thumb she supported her straw,
That stood tall over the glass rim,
Decored helter skelter red stripes on white,
She sipped from the drink's bearing brim.

And deep red gloss filled full her lips.

Watch her smile as she looks across to my eyeline,
With her black-lashed beaming gaze.
Fresh cheeks curve high to a rouged arch,
Her jawline defined through the bar's haze.

She looks away chatting to boss man close by,
Looks back to me and back to him.
Beams white teeth through a mischievous smile,
Her giving thought of us handsome men.

And she giggles with a noted innocence.

...

The liquor bar door opens, the drinkers feel a breeze.
Lady diners look over their men's shoulders,
Gents look back upon themselves to glance,
Town girls entering with giggles for popped-corks,
Tall heels, pretty frocks, handbags from New York.

Barman shakes the cocktails, as women smile with glee,
With low cleavages leaning over the bar,
Deep gloss lips and powdered high cheeks,
Clutching black-pearled purses to high-rouged nails,
Quick winks, lashes black, perfumes by Chanel.

Smell the perfumes by Chanel.

....

Every laugh was infectious with flicked hair,
Every move as she felt her glass,
Long piano fingers with gloss red nails,
Exude an upbringing so middle class.

She then re-touches her lips straight from her bag,
Replaced it and closed the clasp,
Every movement as her fingers cross,
Every thought I have with luscious gasp.

From my stool I walked up and asked of her name,
Stroked from her wrist down to her hand,
Touching to the long tips I adored,
Soft ... meaningful, the ever-wanton man.

I took her hand, held her and longingly kissed lips,
We swayed, clasping each other's waist,
The darkened room led to more passion,
Whispered words, sweet smiles, my heart raced.

Hand to hand, shadows followed
From the wall lights across the floor.
Boss man takes note, then smokes,
Two folded green notes tally his whore.

Upstairs, we promptly paced,
Three folded notes was her request.
Made-payment was always upfront,
Nervous laughter the pay pushed to her breast.


But, this was the early 1930s – the later era of prohibition in the US. The cities' bars lay undercover as alcohol-free establishments, but some run by criminal gangs, were the speakeasies where alcohol was served as reserved.

Blacks were kept out the back, or to the dark of the city night, as the establishments still allowed entry only for whites.


## 3. The Boss

And by the door to the hallway,
Wearing black and white spats,
Braces to his slacks,
Crisp is his open white shirt,
Greased black hair is slicked back.

His charge, three folded notes,
Cheap drugs under his hat,
Moonshine under stools,
In the eerie subdued light,
He's the boss, not nobody's mule.

He will offer you a match lit
In cupped hand to his side.
A gun under the bar,
Flat lips that hardly move,
All men know, not to push him too far.

Two bottles, handed-cash,
A paper bag to cover,
This pimp, later, will trade his lover.

Talking quiet with politeness,
A fresh fat Cuban cigar,
Notes tuck inside his hat,
The speakeasy boss wears
Laced-brogue, New York spats.


4.

The deco building, three storeys-high,
Is the hidden liquored-society.

Walk by and nobody would really know,
Its the drinkers' choice for variety.


## 5. The Downtown Whore

And to the corner of the bar,
Stockings cheap of black,
Stilettos of white,
Cracked lips of red,
We know, she hasn't come far.

Her charge, two green folded notes,
Cott'n sheets of cream,
Closed blinds of white,
The hue of lamp lit,
Men know, she'll hold 'em all night.

A cigarette in long holder,
Stuck gum under the bar,
Half glass to her side,
A donated match light,
She knows, men want her pride.

The flicking of the last ash,
The stubbing out of her fire,
She wants to be, ... every man's desire.

Just a short walk down the stairs,
A pair of fresh bloomers,
Green note tucked in bra,
Fresh gloss lipped-smile,
Men know, she hasn't come far.

Laced, her lady cleavage,
The wanton invited,
Whether rich man, gangster or tar.

**6.**

A flicker in street, wind swept through lights,
A silhouette stood suspicious, by night.

A black Cadillac with darkened glass,
Stares each innocent, that might walk past.

Smoke is blown from the real life bête noire,
Low trilby ... who is the man in the car?


**7. Jazz Man**

Far corner, with hardly a light,
The resident pianist,
Gold tooth to his smile,
He's Moroccan Joseph,
He'll play all through the night.

His fee is two folded notes,
Free lodgings upstairs,
The man lives alone,
Cleans bars by day,
By night, seen stacking the chairs.

His family were the slave trade,
Working fields of sugar beet
Down in New Orleans.
He's a natural player,
The rhythm tapped by his feet.

In a lift of his stool,
One gun, loaded, just in case,
The coolest of guys ... told by his face.

His rhythm is Mississippi,
Blues jazz is his style,
He's 'play it again Jo',
His hands from the land,
Sweet voice, head tilted ... gold teeth to his smile.


**8.**

Across the bar, through the smokiest haze,
Ladies' silver angled holders, raised.

Couples drinking in triangles of light,
Ain't no blacks, entry only for whites.

And four men play with faces for poker,
Have driven far, as they are not locals.

Their babes straighten their stockings tight,
Glam necklines bear black sparkle chokers.


## 9. The Guests

Come through the door from the pavement,
Two men dressed to kill,
Larger brim to trilbies,
Raising as they enter,
They are keen to spot the payments.

The bar entry, one folded note,
Passed low hand to hand.
The tip is the boss man's,
Slipped to his pocket,
The front door, always manned.

Over the bar, one folded note,
Bourbon poured on ice
Ordered in whisper,
Slid over the oak counter,
The sheriff takes his slice.

The two men had never been seen
On Chicago's lanterned-streets,
Where prohibition makes liquor a treat.

The whore smoking at the end bar
Winks to the gents, stoned.
They are from out of town,
Wives at the homestead,
Men should never sleep alone.


## 10.

People under triangular lights,
Now whisper, doors closed by nine.

Order love for sale by quarter past eight,
The queueing wantons served 'til late.

Boss man is keeping his nightly tally,
Tars upstairs with the local sally.

Framed faces hang in subdued light,
Notorietied-gangsters of the night.

The cards are dealt across the table,
Stick matches to baize, bucks out of sight.

## 11. The Wink

She was no Greta Garbo, no Betty Grable,
But a wink and a whistle from one gent,
Two folded notes passed under the table.

Whilst the punter was led up steep wooden stairs,
His friend sat easy, elbows on knees,
Leant forward, drink in hand, toward the door, stared.

Liquor over the bar was passed.

Whispers in triangular light, sparse.

Sound of gunshot from the bedroom, heard ...

The bar gun held in boss man's shaking hand,
After dashing through tables incensed.
The front door unlocked was left unmanned.

Was there a second shot, if not a third?

The gent from his chair held trigger to finger;
Boss man shot point blank, cigar to hand.

....

The waiters' trays flew to the ceiling,
Cocktails flooded over the floor.
Ladies scream under tables, kneeling,

The barman whistling, polishing the glasses
Was saved, the third bullet hit the shade.
Night ladies ran fast from their bar seats.

All this was for whores, profits and liquor.

....

Piano Jo just sat on the loaded gun,
By his smile, you couldn't know his thinking.

....

The jazz piano, broke silence with tinkling.
Who knows from where the brown spat men came?

They had been seen under the Union Loop,
Where their floozies waited for boozies.
If you want truth, they're the Bête Noire sleuths.

Some thought not so ... but many, had their inklings.

The eyes from the gangsters on the wall.

The posters advertised jazz for all.

The deco building has its new owner.

A godfather protected, he's a known loner.

**12.**

Jazz for all.
Liquor for all.
Whores for all.
How the mighty did fall.

Wide-brimmed hats,
Brown-tone spats.
Baggy slacks.
Chicago's street cats.

In the darker corner, piano tinkling.

Ladies with fox fur collars.

Gents with their folded dollars.

They drank along side the tars.

Nobody never wanted no trouble,

But everyone always had an inkling!

# The Seated Man 5

"I can never love,
So will never need."

"I've got my home,
I'm happy being alone."

"Forever, will nature not
Fight holy battles or
Have their Great War ...

...

Wars are the seedlings of man;
Small tribes and creeds that breed
Resentment of their closest neighbour:

From the spears of fear-making-men,
To torches that blazed the hay
Harvested, by other's labours.

The want for the land and its fruits
Made men sail white-crested-waves,
As piranha pirates they'd fight.

In their hundreds, charging horses;
The armour-clad shield armies,
Would joust and sway to slay village gents.

White men making slaves for their flag;
Their bibles, most-liable,
Defending their right of past-revenge."

*"There can never be racial peace."*

"Infantries that pace high hill to field,
Camouflaged as their defence,
To take strong-hold of walled-cities.

Tanks making tracks through dust,
Their scars mark the force-held-state,
The residents begging for bread.

Fired-cannons and incendiaries
Reach to peak over fort-turrets,
The long shot to great devastation.

Planes that take aim at innocents,

The loss of the street-ordinary,
Target-planned to incense,

....

And forefront, the eyes of
Every rogue leader's mind

Is population control ...

Their people, of meagre means,
Will fight their plight for
The podiumed-one, extolled.

Every person, idol-trained,
Yet are down-tamed
So they can never rise against.

They have nothing to lose.
But, the hope of high praise
Raises their aim to further-build:

Another palace,

Another church;

Something they can all look up to."

"Towers and spires stand to be admired."

"There's power to tall windows and flags."

"The grand banners of Big Brother
Look lower to down-trodden-others."

"The centre square crowds,
With their allegiance proud,

Psychologically-mentored
That the world is the enemy.

Not they;
*They* are the innocents;

Scared rabbits with eyes white,
The hunters have them in their sights ...

So fight,

Fight!

Fight!"

....

"Mother Nature builds her own world;
 The birds to the trees,
 Humped whales to oceans,
 Some meat-eaters,
 Some prefer leaves,

 Others scavenge,
 Pigs will hog the lot.

 None are pointing hoof nor paw."

"Never will nature fight a great holy war."

....

"The smoking of coercive smoulder,
 Will ignite as fire, flames fanned to be

 Men's world-destructive ... final great pyre."

....

"There can never be radical peace,
 So, fight, fight, fight!"

"Tamed, drained, to never up-rise."

"Big Brother is their leader,
 There's nothing more the people need."

# Groupers' Hill

The groups are regularly grouping,
Meetings that are now chaired,
For sessions can be broken
If anyone dare be outspoken.

There is now law of the table,
Each group registering a name,
With hands up for democracy.

Presidents.
Chairmen.
Secretaries.

Each comment noted.
Each member voting.

Making non-prejudicial,
Then filed as official.

....

The Go Green campaigners
Are complaining:

There is a tramp making camp
In the woodland of The Dyke.
He's unclean, unkempt,
And not one of them.

The No Bypass Remainers,
Are still un-restrained:

There are too many lorries
Using the road, taking load
Away from the town;
The lanes clogged,

The sun now seen only through smog.

The Mayor and his council
Are now weekly-debating;
Debating more on the table.

He points out government grants,
Received to the treasurer for
Road-tarmacing Skylarks' Park.

The small housing committee,
Point out there are no rooms
For the tramp in the woods.

The office of town planning
Have a butcher applying,
With protest from the bleat-vegans.

**Cricket Pitch Kid**

"What's your name?" asked the playing young child,
And with a manner, mild,
Quick to understand, passed the bat,
And passed the honour front of stumps.

"This is Winston," shouts the giving guy.
Others to the beach
Clap to appreciate the player,
Immediately being one of them.

With bat to the sand, and bent leg forward,
Squinting to the midday sun,
The one instantly promoted-to,
Without rules, may make winning runs.

They are here for the fun.
He toeing the drawn line.

The black batting child, missed a flyer,
Then smashed tip to sand,
Tripped to fall back on the bails.
Even though numb, the others laughed;

They laughed and smiled,
They cheered him on,
And wasn't so long, until ...

Winston hit the ball for six;

The ball that flew the sky.

Higher flying to the blue, it skewed,
As he faster-ran and ran the sands.

And every child endeared him,
He's running line to line.

Again and again the ball pitted
The beach pitch of play,
That lasted all of their days.

The championed-black kid,
Ran to win the last point,
Not even trying to have to prove,
Respect was high-five from every white child.

Black Winston was a friend in an instant.
No prejudice, no thinking,
Nobody had to encourage his smile,
It was always there for each one's taking.

The ice cream cone was his to raise
In his grip high, with biggest grin,
As the trophy for his winning innings.

This was only the beginning ...

Day after day they met on the beach sand,

Together wading and shell hunting,
Together crabbing in pools to rocks,
Each one running to the white of tides.

Winston opened his closed hand,
And shared the little white fan shells
He had found in tens of tens.

Pinched-fingered to give to his friends.

And in the wet of the forebeach,
They imprinted them in curved lines,
That spelled out each of their names.

Laughing in their newly-found friendship,
Smiling through sun-drench long days of play,
Cheering as they run the cricket sand lines.

Winston opened first batting,
And each one knew he'd follow through,
To hit six on six over their heads.

The winning inning was the game's beginning.

He would then fly from sand to catch
Open-handed, with stretch of arm
Against the sky of blue,
The ball to win them that day's match.

"High-five my white friends,
 Ain't it good to be alive."

....

The victory was not his, it was theirs,
As the match, his hand and smile were shared.

....

To his dreams he ran stumps to bowling line,
With the fastest legs,
Reaching the bat, end to end,
Whilst the field defence
Were searching the boundary.

His right arm met the sky,
As he caught the winning ball.

High-fiving as he smiled,
Then giving to his friends.

....

Winston brought other black kids
To stay on the beach of friendship.
Day on day, more and more
Came to play the sun-gazed game.

He was still the champion, and
With friends as companions
They now had a twelve-man-team.

But not all was as it should be ...

The white kids mocked and jeered,
As the black kids played better than they.

The other side won every played-game.
The white guys now drew the new boundary ...

The racial line defined to the ground.

....

To his home town he stood to the towers;
The concrete soured, many floors high.

And the green grass, lawned in between,
Was for practice around the wickets and bails.

He remembered his beach friends,
He thought of the high sixes that sailed ...

Then remembered the whites taunting,
His mind-memories quite haunting.

From the city of prejudice,
The beach of freedom became the same.

History, racial differences, were to blame.

As concrete high rises cut the sky,
Still whites' and blacks' streets were divided.

....

He had learned of the Sugar Beet Road,
His family as slaves behind grand gates.

Freedom still had its paying-price;
Contrast difference of white to black lives.

They sang in cotton pickin' fields,
Each hummed to the shipping loads,

But he couldn't sing for want of thinking.

No score could have been more.

No bat could have hit another six.

No right folk could racially mix.

White men bowled the final lasting wicket.

## The Seated Man 6

"I can feel the wind-of-ill
 That is shaking the trees."

....

"I've seen such devastation
 Of greater nations, that
 Rally and rally to a
 Greater death tally.

 And those who will never talk
 So miss the debating stage,
 Miss the street-heard protests,
 Dissing the point of democracy."

"The so-called land of free will
 Still dines on the bitterest pills."

....

"Within churlish world summit halls,
 All delegates to country, named,
 Are negotiating for the cameras,
 So their points are typed and signed."

"Politely procrastinating,
 Rather than mass-relating."

"Grinding the opposition,
 They are politically taking aim."

"Such, are pros as the juxtaposed,"

"Yet, back-scratching breaks
 Allow shake-deals to be made."

....

"The suit-men have mind-feuded,
 Whilst offending boots line
 Fields around towns for
 The called charge of war.

 The great guns, angle-pointing,
 To enrage the sleeping lessors.

 The empowered leaders desk-kill;
 Drone-planes shadow stilled-beaches ...

 Crosses that are scars to the sky,
 To echo the conscience of each-viewed-eye."

....

"I see Mayor wearing his chain
 As medals he's deserving,
 Yet not even earned them
 To gain the public's respect."

*"There will never be town peace."*

"Every one person, with sound reason,
 Thinks they're their own-cause hero.

 Yet,
 Each one holds their own mind's gun.

 Some join as fellow-comrades,
 Some into battalions,
 Others as complete forces.

 Small tender boats on still waters
 Become grey gun ships to waves.

 The jigsaw pieces that make battles.

 The one missing centre shape,
 Is the trigger of insult to inflame such blame.

 The feeble picture lies to the table,
 Ready to be blown into the air."

....

"The baying cries for war
 Saw a hundred marching the street;
 Arms high, rifles pointing to the sky.

 They weren't from the bigger army,
 In plain clothes and wearing trainers,

 Randomly, with anger to trigger,
 They showed allegiance as they fired ...

 'Allah, Allah, Allah.' They cried.

 The strength of arms punching the air.
 Their shots ricocheted the dark night.

 One wrong move or word could
 See violence break the evening silence.

 This was the faction-rising.
 The actions on these few
 Would affect generations
 Of the majorities, breeding
 Tactics of reactionary carnage.

 Displaying chants for war,
 Like I've never heard before.

 'Allah, Allah, Allah.' They cried."

....

"The staunch residents drowning
  In their tumble-torn town
  Looked through hollowed-windows;
  Looked in horror at the taunts,
  Knowing what then might follow.

  Dreams became nightmares of
  The awoken scared children."

"The women, anxious, ran fraught
  Fingers through scrambled hair."

....

"No moon shone to their demand, brusk.
  The stars to the edging of the night, stayed,
  As to the dark of dark ... *more* darkness, bayed."

....

"A week later saw kidnapping
  Of a schoolgirls' class,
  Each 12 years' old, daylight stolen."

"Stolen in their uniforms
  As their teacher died."

"They as jihadi brides, would marry,
  To serve and breed with older men.

  Radicalised wives.

  They wouldn't be seen again."

....

"The shots ricocheted the town's stark lives."

# Protesters' Hill

The named-groups are now more vocal,
And even though neighbours and local,
Protest with a vengeance,
And are plotting revenge,
So they can all get their way.

The cliques are now gaining donations;
Donations to fight each in elections.

The papers are bulk-printing more press;
Printing to build political factions.

The shopkeepers are closing doors early,
Looking surly, as the local council
Has passed agreement
For a supermarket,
On the edge of the hill –

And 500 car parking!

They are secret-negotiating the man
Who used to hang in the park's trees.
Asking opinion
Of public minions,
With signatures as votes,

Tallying the final tote.

The notes under protesters' stones,
Are suggesting for more weighted-debate.

The Greens now more hill-sighted.

The Remainers are gaining.

Vegans, still bleating reason.

And the Mayor is still holding office;
Neck-holding the glory-gold chain-of-pain ....

Whilst step-hogging The Poppy Memorial,
All groups laid the damned wreath of mistrust.

....

The sour-woman who shouts at clouds,
Is committing her own township treason.
And the petty reason –
More cheaper food prices,
As small stores are price-hiking.

....

Imagine a line of drummer boys,
Climbing up Speakers' for the looming war;
The lead man supporting their flag ...

The War of Absurdity.

Soon will cometh the day.

## The Running Man

I am the ... running man,
Running onward to what I can find,
To never look back over my shoulder,
Scarred by what I have left behind.

What I leave holds such fear,
That haunts with many a tear ...

I am the ...
Man I don't want to be,
The man who fled the scene.

I am the ... cunning man,
Running to find a dark place to hide ...

....

I've seen the search light circle the air,
The trouper that glimpses the night,
That highlights the buildings as square,

That heat-seeks the man on the run.

....

I am the man I don't want to be,
Running the dark of the night.

My quickening breath, shorter in length,
That mists to a plume back past my ear.

The glass of my eyes tells
Such impact of what I dared.

Where no life could've been spared,
The getaway car screeched 'fore I sped.

I am the ... running man,
Now far short of breath,
Sweat pouring from my brow.

With my back to a blank wall,
Caught in a dark dead end.

The helicopter spy to the air.
Its spotlight is on my head.

For I was the gunning man,
That held the trigger tight from behind.
The bank manager with blood to head,
The cashier with tip to her mind,
Queue-customers filled with dread.

Then I quickly to the street fled.

Louder is my shortening breath.
My head bleeds beads of sweat,
Hands running through my hair,
Lipped-mouth quivering, frightened.

I am the ... running man,
The man without a plan,

That yelled at customers lined,
The manager, to the tile floor, dead,
The cashier with crying eyes,
Sawn shotgun filled with lead.

I'm
Crouched at the dark alley's end,
Hoping the dogs lose my scent.

I am the ... cunning man,
With cold and numb hands,

That threw the loot over a hedge,
After pocketing a large note wedge,
That will buy me out of the town,
If they don't first gun me down.

I am the ...
Man I don't want to be,
He who left blood at the scene,

Who cut his hand on counter glass
As the sacked-money was passed.
The cashier with eyes of fright,
The shotgun held with much dread.

....

I hear the sniffer dogs barking;
Barking in the dark of night.

I see the trouper light circling;
Circling, pinpointing its sight.

....

I'm sat back to the wall,
Exhausted, knees bent,
Hand to my head.

Frightened.

Fearful.

So bloody tearful.

I shot a woman and her children dead.

What have I become?

All for money to pay my drugs debt.

....

From county line to line,

To the great chance of doing time.

My name is Winston ... Winston Joseph.

....

I can see my name is spelt on the beach,
I can see me playing the gentlemen's game.

My open hands ... many shells.

Momentarily, I was someone.
My name next to those of whites.

Yet,
The hatred of the racists,
Raised my return-shot aim.

I'm passing bags of *powder white*.

I'm the man ... I don't want to be.

....

My name to be fact on my chest,

Photoed, to ever be on police file.

## Seated Man 7

"For I could never love.
I could never feel,
Nor steal the heart of another."

"So
I do not talk to offend,

Smile to make friends,

Endanger my anger,

Make jealous my eyes.

As,
In the whole of mankind, no honesty lies.

Honesty means truth,
Truth means openness.
Openness means compassion.
Compassion means love.

And to not blend with
Others close to me ...

My sadness can be best company."

"In the whole of mankind, *no honesty lies*."

"Straightforward are my eyes,
Even though danger pries to
The side, above ... and behind.

I will just talk to reply,
Never remark defensive, so
Every word as polite."

"My hands never raised,
My voice stays as low,
All thoughts processed slow."

"If I stand to another man,
My eyes will meet his own,
And repeat ... my long past history."

"As, any expression leaves an impression;
Somebody's smile can rile another."

"As one sporting side cheers, the other will jeer."

"For every big win, to another, ... the loss is larger."

"And, ... if I cry, it's not for myself,
It is for humanity, ... that is in denial."

"In the whole of mankind, no honesty lies."

....

"Peacetime was a temporary pause
To conflict as humanity's cause.

Each side showed their full strengths,
Each manned with eyes of contempt.

Losses were so many hundreds,
Whole towns were downed as rubble.

The allies brokered a two-state-deal;
For Holy Month, the fighting ceased."

....

"The dust settled day after day,
The streets still lay there, as bare."

....

"The men suddenly felt delayed trauma,
Adrenaline had run through their veins ..."

"Month after month, they, hardly sleeping,
The whole drama re-ran through their minds."

....

"My hands had never felt as raw,
As we removed rubble to front doors.

Then I looked inside ...

There laid a wife and child;
Arms clinging, frightened to the floor,

Their bodies char-black-burnt,
Their clothes were scorched,

... No skin to their faces – opened-jawed."

....

"I've touched bodies where souls had left,
Touched the shoulders of the huddled-bereft,
Felt the tears of my great fellow-soldiers,
Saw the Gates of Heaven before I was dead."

"*I saw Heaven* ... before I was dead."

....

"That child cried as his mother was dying,
 To then take the Pathway to Allah,
 So innocent, ... for all the wrong reasons."

....

"Day after day, the town in settled-dust,
 But ... to the air ... was the stench of distrust."

....

"The men slouched, collapsed to heaps,
 What had occurred beyond their belief.

 The other side to steal religious pride,
 The fought-for-land, between flags, divided.

 With worn out-faces to the sky,
 Disbelieving-mouths agape,
 They cried, as I've never seen crying;

 Down-mouths curved to cheek sides,
 They choked their spit, for family, died."

....

"Then after call to prayers across the lines,
 They steeled their self-pitying-pride,

 Stepped over their dead-slayed
 That had yet to be placed to graves,

 Took their arsenal to clenched hands,
 Passed rifles to their fellow-fighters,

 The war again re-started ... before the
 End date of cease-fire was made."

....

"Before *the others* broke the held-trust,
 This side plumed their holy prayers to dust."

*"Plumed their prayers ... to dust."*

"Eye for an eye ... the others were to die."

*"There will never be Middle East peace."*

....

"Peacetime was a temporary pause
  To conflict as humanity's cause."

"Conflict *is* humanity's cause."

....

"I've touched bodies where souls had left,
  Touched the shoulders of the huddled-bereft,
  Felt the tears of my great fellow-soldiers,
  Saw the Gates of Heaven ... before I was dead.

*I saw Heaven* ... before I was dead."

# Banners' Mount

Look up from pretty town,
For the historical Speakers' Mount
Is now banner-adorning.

Each group, each committee
Has its own hoarding,
To allow them to speak out.

Even the council were revoked,
By groups who threaten
To rescind their needed-vote.

....

Ms. Tourette's is still shouting;
Shouting she can no longer be seen,
Because the covering posters are sprouting.

The grass feeders are planning;
Planning to pull down the banners,
As they are produced from nastiest plastic.

The bypass remainers complain;
Complain that the many road users
Can see the vast boardings when driving through.

The farce-council have another plan ...
The Mount can make money from advertising
To 'promote' town and new motorway services.

And the man who sat in the tree,
Is canny of his next plot of anarchy.

This, the town of undered-diversity.

**The Lives Of Men**

**The Man On The Edge**

With bare hands he has climbed
To the ledge on the edge of face.

Standing tight, his back to the crags,
His feet overhang the rock's crop.

He's looking down at the fall of doom,
With Hell's waves baiting his drop.

....

It was a nice day to the sun's rays,
But the sea's storm is bounding.

....

His dare-hands now clench behind,
Arms tight to his side, stands frozen.

They ooze blood from their cuts,
The wrong cliff face has been chosen.

He can't look up his grief's sheer,
His neck can't check his progress.

He can side-creep a little right,
He can side-reach slightly left.

The storm won't be long coming,
The sea's spray's spitting at his face.

....

He recalls all his days from the past,
But are deemed to be drowning.

....

For The Man Who Stands Crisis' Edge
Didn't chose to climb all his life.

To have to hike higher could become dire.
The clamber down would be a slip on his cliff.

....

And when all turns dark,
He can mind-see hunting sharks.

....

He can inch a little to the left,
He winces a step to the right.

Each thought, each moment,
Is the balance of life's parts.

Others have freedom of chance,
They ride the tide to where they go.

But not he.

He is stranded. From others, disbanded.

He's clenching the cracks to his back,
Life's sea pitting to his eyes.
Insulting wind to both ears,
And hair pulled by the bully storm.

He's standing on the ever-knife edge.
One day he'll jump ... but doesn't know when.

Every thought, his heart is pounding.

The net of religion can catch his fall,

... It's mankind's safety for the lives of all.

# The Night Owl

Is he the wise one?

When the town bars close,
All have gone home,
And lamps glisten to night drizzle,

He awakens.

When the last few revellers'
Echoed-laughs bound the air,
Their footsteps fade to the shade,

He is the man from the shadows;

The man who walks the night,
Counts each hour by the bells,
That spell all is quiet ... and all is well.

He reads yesterday's papers,
Discarded to the street-side seats,
To know what has been, whilst he slept.

Peers tomorrow's early news,
From the van drop to the local store,
To know what will be, whist he dreams.

And knows the weather before the light of sky.

Ask The Man Who Lives By Night why,

He will tell you,

"I can know more about the people,
 Without being *with* the people.
 More about the day ahead before bed,
 And more about yesterday, as it fades."

"Those who are wise, only use their eyes."

"Only those that have peace, have time to think."

"And as I walk the street,
I have not to share,
I have not to care,

 Not to speak, nor hear,"

"And the whole of the town, the world,
 The night that energises my mind,

 Is mine."

....

He doesn't want to be part of the headlines,
No thought to be in society's headlights,

But just to know where it is going,
And where it has been,
And what he foresees it will be.

He doesn't need the day's sun,
Just to know that it is dawning.

Only those who are wise, use just their eyes.

## The Man In The Lighthouse

What is he searching for?

He climbs two hundred stairs,
Spiralling the walls of his world;

A world that allows him to go
Higher; higher than many others,

Yet, he stands to his future, vast.
Stands with glass-spread hands,
And eyes that can magnify.

And as the mind light turns,
It momentarily glimpses;
Glimpses his far-off horizon.

Every week, month, year,
He tries to see more clearly;
What is possibly out there.

Spiralling up two hundred stairs,
And with his mind despaired
He descends the same lines.

Nobody can stand beside him.
Nobody to hold his hand in
His narrow spiralling world.

What is he searching for?

He can always inch a thought
Of what lies to the darkened-sky,
Star-dotted to his onward-path.

But there is nothing he can see,
Nothing that sits as a ship
On the horizon's vastest sea.

His view?
Is his seeking beam of hope.

Hope that in him, forever remains.

But his thoughts and dreams,
And beliefs are a descending slope.
So, to stand to the future,
Is the only way that he can cope.

All that can be his,
Glimpsed around 360 degrees.

The stars are constantly, cloud-marred.

Many others stand to their self-cliff face,
But he could be the hope of his race.

If you met The Man Of Beaconed-Hope,
In his eyes there is constant glare

- Nothing in his distanced-stare.

**The Courthouse**

A cough echoed the court,

And who would have thought
That, ... one man was to hold the show.

With head wigged, blowing gown,
As though he has flown in
To the dock house of the sinners.

Now let him begin.

The silence in the jury;
Innocent as sideshow ducks,
That can be knocked back
By the renowned truth-shooter.

The gavel to the table lies.

The court silenced awaiting
His first theatrical clause ...

A nod to the judges,
Introduction to the jury,
He's using seduction,
Throwing bread for his cause.

They are quick to lap up.

For the accused is to testify,
Through questioning, clevered,
He was in the wrong, crime-scened,
And his fingerprints taken,

And he's not police-mistaken.
They just want his back-bacon.

A three second pause.

The wall clock hour-ticked.

Again, with low of head,
Reading his pretend script,

The bluff to hold his laud,

And if the actor was allowed applause,
He would have bowed to the crowd.

As a driver to the straight road of law,
Some foot the kerb of innocence,
Yet he swerves and meanders,
Crossing them to the guilt-ridden path.

You might quite laugh!

But the man with hands to wheel,
Has in his rear-view mirror
A trail of prejudiced, justified roadkill.

Contempt of law as the slaughter.

Even though the stand taken,
You'd be mistaken, as it is
Not centre-stage to the theatre.

The man in the wig
Is the host to the show,
And with pointed, shiny toe,
Will walk and talk the aisle.

Gesturing, gesticulating,
Pompous, his gait,
Thumb under brace,
Churchill's, bow-laced.
Spectacles, half to his nose.

Looking over their rims,
Is a look of supposing,
He's to start the great show.

A pause, ... the inevitable cough.

The sideshow duck line sit back,
Now, no longer quack-relaxed.

A jester of time-reminiscence,
The court clock points, hand-straight,
Then with a gist of his wrists,
Wanded-stick, his lines of contortion ...

The perceived-mind of the crime.

Now,
The cards shouldn't be shown racist,
But in the upstanding court of law,
Across the jury, behind the gavel,
And the lawyers to the slaughter,
The man to the stand, cuffed-hands,
Is the only black face – in the whole place.

*The only black face – in the whole place.*

His eyes shifting to each wall,
Then to the judges, to the jury.
You can feel his nerves, mind-disturbed,

As verbalising hands of the host
Lie open to suggestion,
Knuckle-fist pointing
Allows him to apply pressure,
Then a slight raise of voice,
And implying-reiteration.

The accused mind's confused,
With words clevered, some absurd.
Some said slowly and lowly,
As pretence to being patient.

The air dries to a bone, as members,
Side by side, cough as infectious.
They are scribble-writing,
And quite rightly, his words spoken spritely.

Almost Shakespearean, the actor
Is the only benefactor of today's show.

That's how it goes!

Four hours to the last scene,
The summary to the curtain fall.
The jury preside to the room behind.
The accused moved as prisoner,
To sweat and regret his answers.

The jury return shuffle-seating,
To their precised-position for the decision.

"All stand!" The officer demands,
As the truth judges, humble, together mumble.

For,

The white majority, voted priority,
That the black guy should do time for crime.

His crime? Is completely sublime;

For he remonstrated to the white police,
Who arrested Winston, on drug charges.
To his neck, lay one of their knees.
Fast gasping, he was unable to breathe.

*Last gasping* ... he was unable to breathe.

The officer may be sacked, job-losing,
The guy's family in psychological tatters.
Now the whole community play as jury,
To the streets they have demonstrated ...

As,
Black lives matter!

## Seated Man 8

"We walked and walked to the nearest shore,
No mission accomplished, onward home,
Our legs tired, backs were sore,
We stood to the soft of dunes.

Our mind's were stoical from what we saw,
There were no heroics borne on our tour,
From walking forward, faced with war,
We learned to see both sides."

"Don't just look one way,
... There's always two sides."

"Two hundred troops as comrade-platoons,
We heard ally ships blow to the mist,
Funnel ghosts as they approached,
We were now ... on our way home.

Filing two by two,
Over the smooth of the beach
To the toe-edge of the sea,

Urchins bobbed to waves,
Reaching shore, then
Pulled back again.

I picked one up,
And packed it
To my rear rucksack.

That one was for luck,
My souvenir packed.

As the ships' anchors lowed,
Tenders launched, no longer alone.

Our comrades to outward row
Twelve men to the bobbing boat –
We looked back ...

Still, missiles arced the skies,

Billows of smoke choked
Stoned-temples and homes.

And in my vacant eyes,

The women, out-laying hands,
Eyebags drooped to cheeks
That had never been wetter.

Their wailing mouths,
Grief-rounded chins."

"This, the war, nobody would win."

"The bell to its arch, as a heart,
  That could beat no more."

"The local felled sign read 'girls and boys'."

"The domes as skeleton bones."

"And dust that lay over every man's face,
  Same lay ... smothering every dead's grave."

....

"The hundred year war that
No hero ... could *ever* save,

So we left feeling desperately low."

....

"Never to forget,
  Slain corpses lined by the road;
  No epitaphs, nobody's names."

*"Peace can never be universal."*

"I've trudged through torn towns,
  Carrying comrades to back,
  Lowered them to graves
  With eyes died,
  Cheeks, concaved,
  And arms splayed,
  As where they lay ...

The same men stood starboard
To wave their families goodbye
As the portside band played,
To return again ... another day."

"Each one, a wanten hero."

....

"The nuclear mushroom cloud,
  Held as a red button threat,

From despots playing games,
Each politically taking aim,

Each accumulating their score,
Through brutal combat,
Nerve gases to masses,
Culling mountain factions,
As allowed religious action."

"No wonder the human race
Is more than deplorable."

....

"For those in plight for peace,
The game is more than brutal;

Each one fighting incitement
To their thriving, quiet lives.

Each will never be heroic,
Yet each, ... was prepared to die."

....

"I've stood behind doors
Before the enemy entered;
Rifle to chest,
Chin to neck,

*Holding my breath
Until they had left.*

I've laid across roofs,
Bombed army pounds,
Climbed field trees,
Bullet rounds loaded.

As close cars exploded,
The force of air balling
Knocked doors through,
Blew people to ground.

Found grassed-live mines,
Barbed-wired snares,
Fork-tongue-snakes,
Scorpion tails.

*A wink of my eye
I could have died.*

Yet, could have been blinded
By tear gas attacks,
Pepper spray-choked,
Chemical-burned.

Each day was a lesson learned,
Covering our tracks,
Diving in water,
Periscopes over.

We were window-glass showered,
Thrown-petrol bombs, blown,
That crazed a trail,
Flames raging high.

*The grease on my face,*
*Saved scorch from the blaze.*

Witches were burned,
Thought-guilty were stoned,
Men hooded for hanging,
Guillotined to the throat,

And their commanding leaders
Wore medals to their chests.

The cowering crowds
Psychologically kept down."

"The scars to my mind
Can never be blinded."

"Each memory is stored."

"Each image never removed;

Babies dying for water.

Women praying to God.

Yet, ... men ... kept killing in war."

...

"The child brides, they'll never find.

Their families ever un-reconciled."

....

"The dust might settle end of a day,
But the next ... would bring the very same."

....

"No man or crowd will be
Ever-cowed by the supremacists.

The taking of lives
Or land is most divisive intimidation.

No nation should have to
Be slain into underclass submission."

"The ships and planes
Have ever tamed arrows and spears.

Constant fears through
Generations keep the people in line.

But, watch the new thought rising.

Watch arrows becoming barrelled-guns,

That will become cannon fire."

*"There will never be classless peace."*

A new movement will be found,
They, not to remain as put-downs.

Then to be backed by ally forces
That will break borders for battle.

No war will ever be a private affair.

The cameras, the journalists, stand there.

Watch the supremes' smiles' beam.
They have the world's focussed-lens."

"They are supported by trodden-men,
Who will fight, or lose their own lives."

....

"I've sat with families to ask why,
Even through prayer – patience,
Tolerance and acceptance were denied.

But even when one group were
Overwhelmed to surrender,
Another's factors brewed in the hills."

....

"Humanity has its mind's jury
  That sits to judge what it sees."

"The gavel lies in its eyes."

"Love and peace seated
  Lower than envy and jealousy –
  That have built their attraction
  With hatred and greed.
  Happiness apron-stringed to
  The ever-created sadness,
  While contentment's dormant,
  Never to be in the ruling."

....

"I remember the empowering twin towers
  Becoming giant broken trophies.

  The glory pieces will always be
  Another group or country's emotives.

  What is one nation's definition,
  Can be another's inflammatory."

"How long can Liberty uphold her torch?"

"*How long* can Liberty uphold her torch?"

....

"The world needs one flag
  That flutters and flaps to rising sun.

  Billions singing in harmony;
  The words as a universal anthem,

  Where the young do charity as duty ...

  No gods.
  No churches.
  No religions.

  No books of peace,
  That build libraried-wars.

  ... And pay homage to their ancestors,
  Without resentment of the cause fought,
  Or possible radicalised-thoughts.

  For the building of an idealistic tradition
  Will always breed man-conditioning.

So life is for living,
And death is final.

Beyond, there *are* no idols,
That seed-sow battles of attrition."

....

"Live your life beyond any religion,
You'll neither be a saint nor sinner."

"It doesn't take *just* the barmy
To lead assault of conflict armies."

....

"Make yellows, blacks and whites,
Actually build the same road ...

The road to Everyman's Mountain;
The mountain that touches the sky.

To imagine as you sit up upon high,
Beneath you, an Alpine-range
Holds every man,
Every woman,
Every child,
Your mother, your father –

Each and every one buried inside."

"To think on Humanity's Cause Peak,
Nothing's above you;

No perceived mind-thought of love
Of faith as your sight.

Everything is below,
For every kind to bestow.

Humanity's Loss Hill that holds every man's grave,
And beholds ... everyone's name.

An eternal ridgeline of poled-flags, half-mast,
That grieve rich white man, black men, poor.

No colours to their motifs and creases."

"It's only when we die, we become the same;
Equal, ... side by side, ... facing the same way."

....

"Live your life beyond religion,
  You'll neither be a saint nor sinner."

"*There is nothing* above you."

....

"No rose will grow through
  Humanity's age-cracked-walls."

"No petal will spell
  A truce to man's lacking-cause."

"No small seed will feed
  Peace to the wanting many ...

Round turrets stand
As commemoration ... to the buried."

....

"Every man thinks he's a hero.
Each holds his own mind gun,

Yet his barrels loaded,
Will head-on, meet another's."

....

"Sympathy, empathy are
  Remembered ... just temporarily ...

As the peace-cortège quickly passes,
Heads are momentarily lowed for the show.

The memory-flowers by only a few thrown.

... The stems have no strength
To animosity's historical length."

....

"The souls of the dead
  Haven't just left ... they have hurriedly fled."

"See them look quick-back,
  The whole of mankind still fighting ...

They were the lucky ones
Who got out while the heavens
... Still have a few places left."

"Divided families mourn their death –
 Such devastated hearts to the theft,

 They were the lucky ones … "

"The heavens have … just … a few places left."

….

"For every grain of dust
 Isn't just sand of immemorial-time,
 Broken beyond religious-dates,

 But the damage from each side's mistrust."

"In own-tears of disgust ….

 Men's dead wives and children lay,
 On wind-brushed bedding … their history made."

….

"By Allah, stand to be judged.
 Let's hope he commends your action.
 No defendant can take condemnation."

"In the destruction of other men's lives,
 Through mosque-sanctioned-prayers,

 *Let's hope* … he commends your actions."

….

"Every grain of dust,
 Is
 The breakdown of their long history's trust."

**The Jail Cell**

Stripped of his dignity,
Winston sat to his bunk.
This, the time for his thinking.

The boy on the beach
Would and could never be
The white man's friend.

For all his great wanting,
A smile that welcomed,
And hands that played,

He was *only* their holiday toy.

That trophy golden cone held
In the sun ... was just wafer-thin.

But his legs ran and ran,
And his mind replayed the joy.

....

On the cricket pitch of green,
The stadium should be
The common-ground church,

But
There are still two battle teams,
Even within the ring boundary;

The bowler as attacking,
The cavalier soldiers to the field,
Each batsman as defender,
Strip-umpires to judge,

And the bails balanced
As the scales of justice
On wicket-pillars of disparity.

He and his friends momentarily won.

They were crowned as so.

But beyond the playing stadium,
There was the *greater* cricket pitch of life;

Mostly white men were judges.

Pale skins to the police.

Blond hair, blue eyes in the jury.

"Even The Lady of Justice,
  That high-adorns every court,
  Is Caucasian.

Her scales ain't balanced,
Her covered eyes aren't blind.

She is not standing on *our* streets,

But branding as the umbrella of *her* society."

There was the dream, his grandparents saw,
1963 – The Lincoln Memorial;

"Martin Luther hailed every black man's thoughts;

That they should have equal pay, equal rights,
Equality for everyman's jobs,
That weren't just the land for the whites."

He, again, spelled hope out loud.

"We stood to our TVs for Mandela,
Held hands for Barack's inauguration;
First black president in US history."

"Hope and faith together became great.
Over the nation, he hit six on six."

"The championed of the cricket pitch,
Not just running bails to bails,
But tipping his bat state on state."

....

"But the prejudice has beaten me,
That I have to run faster;
Run faster to keep up
With my fellow countrymen."

"Not running the sand or streets,
But sinking in mud under my feet."

"We are generations on from my
ancestors, whose babies were
Named Hope, Faith and Charity."

"Today, they could be Christened –
Nope, Blame and Shame."

"I've tried, I don't deny, to have
More of the white folk's traits."

"But that ain't me."

....

"I spelt my shell-name to the beach.
I was someone next to those of whites.

The same now scribed plaque-to-chest,
In front of the height line wall."

"Look at the sighs to my fallen eyes.

Photoed, to ever be on police file."

....

"The same sighs are there for life –
Instead of success from hope,
... In *every* black folks' eyes."

**The Seated Man**

**The Love Swan**

As the apples bobbed to the water's edge,
In the cold morning mist
The pens and cobs fed.

Their white bodies seen as haze silhouettes,
Save for orange bills to their heads.

Fine mist as a duveted-bed.

The leaves sparsely floating
On the stilled-lake for boating.

Dabbling to the weed,
Dabbling to the reeds.

Ghostly, the lines of their necks.
Silence, save for the feeding.

Dibbing in the weed,
Dibbing in the reeds.

They bill-nudged the windfalls,
Before they open-pecked;
Straight, their low, long, necks.

Ambling in the mist,
Rambling The Dyke's edge.

They fished to the river's bed;
One swoop with feathered-tails to air.

Dipping to below,
Dripping beads to heads.

....

As the sun hued the mist rising,
Some floated to preen under wings,
Some stood, to clean ruffled-breasts,

Each with a curve of their necks.

Then all to the water,
One cob with flap of wings,
Took to fly ...

His cumbersome body,
Heavy to the air,
His feet slapped the water.

As he flew to low,
The others followed so ...

The pageant of white swans,
As though masts so high,
Became a squadron flying the opaque sky.

An angle, slight as they flew;
Flap of white wings,
Slap of wide feet,
They clapped the water
As they cried.

Then the rush ... of feathered-air,
A pulse, so strong ... to their flight.

*The hush* of brushed air.

Grey crosses lapping through the mist,
With necks long as they stretched,

As though some great magical sight.

They disappeared to the east,
Into the haze of yellowed-rise-light.

....

But one swan was left to the water;
One of the many daughters.

For she was the pen with the broken wing.

As the man sat under the trees,
She clumsied onto the bank.
He started to shuffle back.

So cautious of her approach,
Worried as she walked as slow,
Defensive,
Her shoulders up, her head to low.

But he, seated statue,
As she stood to his feet,
Then offered his arm;
Slow to forward-reach,
His hand shaped as head and beak.

In a paused quiet moment,
Autumn mist low to the roots ...

No squirrel scampered.
No magpie claxoned.
No laughter of jester ducks.

The last of leaves slowly fell.

... Her body stance then lowed,
Her neck to his friendship hand, bowed.

She snorted a soft blow;
Highlighted cold to sun's glow.

Kind-rubbing the man-cob beak
With the side of her bill,
Up and down, along its length.

The start of love so bestowed.

Rubbing hand to head,
Loving ... with no words said.

*Silence blissed in the mist.*

Then slow to rise to crouch,
He offered, doubting, his head,
Nose out-pointed as a snout.

She rubbed cheek to cheek,
Loving, ... no words to speak.

She honked to low.

He nose-slow-blowed ...

....

His heart felt the flight of angel swans
That danced to the air with necks, longed,
Upright with lit-candle bills.

Their wings to their backs,
The heavens opened to sing.
Feathers highlighted to choral song.

....

Her head to his cheek,
His hand to comfort her need.

Then the love of a pursed-kiss.

*The secret hidden to the mist.*

.....

The pen with the broken wing.
The man-cob with his gestured ring.

His love swan walked land to water
With toppling feet.
She looked back to find her man.

Proud was her tall of neck,
Her eyes smiled as she turned her head.

"Come with me." ... No words were said.

The man over-awed,
Followed slowly on all fours.

"Come with me." ... His fast heart was led.

She crouched to the water,
To look back with her neck as an S.

"Follow me."

Slowly, he pawed.

Breast-first she took to the lake,
He then hand-dived in the cold of morn.

A flutter of her wings,
To spiral and splash,
She upright, again,
With head beads of wet.

She flirted with her lover.

He too, spiralled to water,
To then tread in the shallow depths.

With nose to bill,
And an arch of her breast,
Backward, the curve of neck,
Their swan-love heart was made.

Both gently to blow,
Their breaths steamed in cold air.

Her wings rose as a flirt,
He copied, winged-arms paired.

Then a touch to her velvet head.
A loved hand from her nape,
He felt the long curve of her neck.

Over damp feathers, his fingers led.

And wet beads balled upon her bill.

To orange, a clear ball tear,
That magnified the woodland trees,

That mirrored the sky,

Reflecting his whole life.

With flat hand to her chin,
With gentle lips, *the tryst in the mist.*

"Follow me." He took to the water
To then take a swim.

She followed not far behind.

In the silence of the Sunday air,
The wake of water, fanned in lines.

....

Her family returned as a squadron strong,
The cobs to defend their young pen,
To attack presence of evil man,
Thinking something could be wrong,

Triangular feet whooshing, as water brakes,
To fast-swim towards the lovers.
Breasts low-hulled to the water,
Pushing forward with fast-paddle legs.

Attacking with bills wide agape.
Attacking with bills that hissed.

Her lover, urgent, escaped along the lake.

The fury of white cobs at war,
The flurry of white battle ships.

Their wings as sails to propelling wind.

In the shallows the man-cob turned,
Attacking back with arm wings high,
Attacking back, honking his lips.

The flurry of white feathers torn,
The fury of the man-cob's fist.

....

To the depths the war swans returned,
Receding back ... with their heads low,
Receding back ... the pen was spurned.

There was a silence to the morn.

Calm again, he, king-cob crowned.

....

The man-cob's head low to the water,
Under comforting wing of his lover.

With gentle feathers wrapping his head,
The pen-lover pressing wounds that bled.

She dabbling with wet bill lips,
Mouth-poured to open wounds of red.

....

The seated man had found love.
His mind and world complete.

His pen bride slept along side,
Each night
By her man-cob,
With one window,
With one door,
And a shared heart.

This,
All that he wanted ... from the very start.

## The Future Vision

Sunday midday the Bypass Remainers climbed the hill,
Louder than loud, placards to up high.
They marched, journalists behind.

Sunday, half twelve, the Grass Feeders ascended Speakers',
Prouder than proud, protesting the butcher,
They marched, with cleavers to hand.

Sunday, nearly one, Mayor and council drove the Hill of Free Choice,
Chauffeured, the township voices to endear,
To hear the thoughts of detesting men ...

Impressive, fine robes and chains,
Dressed, with upstanding importance.

Sunday, past one, the lady who shouts at clouds climbed,
With resounding clout, sweeper brush fanned.
If she could fly on broom, would get there sooner.

The Mayor took all acrimony felt,
Cowed to voices,
Faced placards,
Threatening weapons.

With hands flat, asking them to abate,
It was too late,
The insults
Were never lessening.

As, to the hill, black men paraded,
Last minute wading into the fray,
With mighty fists up, combined,
Playing the racially-motivated card.

"We are."
"We are."
"We are."

The Mayor, related to ancestor-uncle
Who ruled the sugar beet slaves,
Was pelted and pelted with the
Weighting-stones, forcefully thrown.

Violence raged over hope.

The Vegans threw pigs trotters,
The Remainers covered him in oil,
The Greens showered him in leaves,
Whilst punching the butcher serving sausages.

Speakers' Hill became Riot Mound,
Everyone trolled the Mayor's council,
Every clique fought every other clique,
Democracy was now overwhelmed.

Violence stood at the storm's helm.

....

Then,
One man stood on Proclaimers' Box
In the noise of the hundreds,
And held his arms above, finger wands,
To calm the weather of the town.

Everyone stopped.

Few words were spoken.

Nobody knew from where he had come,
He didn't climb Speakers' with every other.

But,
Each person; woman, child,
Black and white,
Witnessed the resurrection of

The Man Who Held The Sky.

He told of the church of friendship
And with lending wise words,
Sold how they could all pray the same way,
All kneel the same direction,
With 'Order As Their Shepherd'.

To hold linked-hands to understand.

The crowd looked at each other dumbfounded.
Some put their weapons down, and walked
To the town to celebrate their differences.

The shoulder-dove's spreading wings
Cast affection that could become love.

The bugle of hope, played to the slope.

....

Again, you could hear crickets sing to clear nights,
Fight-battle ships became row boats to The Dyke,

The hands-chained became a statue
Above the Justice Court of Kindred Skins,

While, to neighbouring-porches,
Black guys, humming whilst strumming.

And by Millennial Rock on Whispering Hill,
A marble figure standing,
With arms out, fingers wide,

To
The Man Who Held The Mound's Pride.

The town had a new church-of-thought,
A new set of bells would ring amongst others.

Every man would learn to be a brother.

....

There are the leaders as feeders,
And those, hands cupped, to be fed and led –

Accepting of the holy, tongue-melt bread.

The body, the words of Christ, makes suffice.

The pews are there for the kneeling,
Laid feather-light pages
Bound in leather, for prayer.

Heralded-words to enthuse the needy.


Let others criticise and think twice ...

From the plague-noise of outside,
The stained glass lights ... the 'perfectly-quiet'.

Be mind-led below the fed-tab bread.
Sip-lips to bled-chalice wine.

There's order In the shepherd cd flock.

But the telling bells of peace
Would some day cease,

As this born-religion will grow to fight its cause,
As those ... that have ever done so, before.

The minorities vocally-dismiss the
Democratic-vote-made majorities.

Order be the shepherd of the blinded-few,
But, beyond the pews ... it, will not be everyone's view.

## Society's Song

As a child I sang;
I sang alone, out of tune.

As a teenager I sang;
I sang against the elders' choir.

As a man I learned to sing;
Sing with concerted-society.

But society's song wasn't *my* song,
So I wrote inspired words,

And again, sang alone.

My song wasn't society's song,
So I sang louder;
Louder to my own stage.

Society didn't hear my own song,
So, disenchanted, the words
Became *my* chant.

Some people heard my chant.
It became *their* song, and so sang along.

With patience of time,
The chant became a descant for the world,
That became a melody for all,
To become an anthem.

The whole world sang together;
People upon people,
Nations upon nations,

From few written words ... on a single scrap of paper.

# Remembrance Hill

And all future generations learned
The history of their home town;

How it grew,
The stories of Speakers'-
The quiet democracy hill
That became an uncontrollable mountain.

The councillors not written in,
The clique groups were un-named,
Except ... black folk who gained hope-rights.

The field, relaid as a road,
That became a services-motorway
Was always written as a success.

But,
Beyond all the mis-writings,
Each celebrated to remember
The man who never gave his name,
Only his number;

He who fell in love with the Dyke Wood swan –

The man who sailed seven seas,
Trekked highest mountains,
Flew the bluest skies,

Yet,
Never felt, in his modesty,
To proclaim on Speakers' Hill.

Private to captain to hero,
With one set of clothes.

And to the river bank, a written-plaque,
As being a man for the world;

The man with no plan,
As ... all plans are damned.

One possession,

But many a thought.

No longer ignored;

No longer appalled by the town, ... he so deplored.

....

Partial paraplegic, he sat to the bank.

From the emotion to his face,

That bore the years,

Thought-peoples' fears,

Cried trauma-ed tears,

The harsh, physical souvenir;

His lower legs ... did a lot less,

And, told a little more
Of his whole Force's life ... not sold.

....

You might have asked the man,
Who's eyes, many memories held,

"When and where did you lose
 The ability to properly walk?"

He would search his history;
Search the stills in his mind –

The black and whites,
That quick-glimpse his thought:

The turrets standing tall,
The women distraught,

Children, choke-hiccupping as
They scream-cried by doors;

They were to be orphans,
From the invading onslaught.

The anger of revenge-men,
With their mighty fists, clenched.

A world where nobody smiled,
Nobody shook friendship-hands,
No kisses or love of one's wife,
Except ... when clinging dear life.

... But then,
The moment ... he could not find.

Blinded from his conscience ...

He remembered running coarse grass,
Looking back at the bombs and shells,
His comrade was along his side,

Who trod on a guerilla's mine,
The earth was ruptured in the blast,

The man hastened forward,
Looking back, his brother was dying.

He also fell with shattered legs.

*That moment* ... he could not find.

....

All heroes sometimes cry;
Cry for what they have witnessed ...

The savages of war.

The mass loss of innocents.

Conflict of creeds and castes.

Humanity's reflective-flag should ever be half-mast.

... And even more for what onward lies.

....

Whispering Hill won't stay quiet too long.
Wait for the new thought-speakers
Who will eventually raise their voices,
Braze their stance, display placards higher,

Until history repeats on The Hill of Free Thought.

....

Peacetime is a temporary pause.

Everyone thinks they're a championing-hero.

.

# Repeated Man

Please be seated and understand
The epitaph echoed to the heroed-man:

"The cross-bridges to forts are drawn,
  Roped-tight to the higher stones.

There, not just stopping impending war,
  But keeping out each millennia, fought."

"Bare boardroom tables are there for debate,
  But it seems all have entered too late ..."

"Every man thinks he's his own cause,
  Their subtlety as history's Trojan horse."

"They are attacking other's self-plauded walls;
  The walls that are beliefs they ever hold."

....

"Every one who ever held a gun,
Hasn't won.
Just a used number –
They ever-remain unsung."

"Their fathers might be proud,
  But each mother will hold self-console."

....

"I, never escaping from the pain
  Of the Women With Wailing Mouths."

....

"I've witnessed shear devastation –
  Death, the multiplied calculation."

"The rose of truce has no use."

"Look at the graves ... without a single name.
  Their heritage to never bring shame ...

Peacetime will ever be a temporary pause,

  ... And, all sides instilled ... the very same."

"If the others don't hold the framed-mind,
  They gather together with pointed-shout –

Blame, blame, blame!"

....

"Allow fellow man his independence hill
  And he will then serve you no ill."

"Flags are the tag above the common hold,
  That fly allegiance in their colours, flown."

"Keep yours flying to you and your own.

  Your mast doesn't deserve every man's fold."

....

"There are no winners in worlds destroyed ...

Too many 'heroes' are self-serving,
Their deserving mis-honestly told."

"And they all want to be applauded."

"Few fighting-wars are ever endorsed."

"Never will nature fight ... *its* great holy war ...

  Yet, destruct *is* humanity's cause."

"Destruct is humanity's cause ...

  Humanity's cause,"

....

"Walk the street of peace,
  The hardest demand is to understand.
  Offer your hands across open bridges."

....

"Through religions, stealth, wealth,
Difference to others' skin colours,
Political persuasions,
Land, minerals, raw materials ...

In this beautiful-natured world,

Your legacies are built on jealousy,
Animosity or conspiracy.

A rear-view of atrocities."

....

*"There will never be agreed peace."*

"Destruct is Humanity's Cause."

And what are you doing with *your* lives?

Are you applauding Everyman's Mountain?

Saluting up to every land's flag

Knowing the view for the future

Is to respect every person's sky?

....

Hum the world's anthem,
From fields, through cities, to seas.

Then learn the words, heard,
And sing in the choir of choirs.

Thrive in everyone's life.

....

Until then, faith and hope will always be in our scope.

Everyday, we will anticipate impending bad weather.

Life's challenges are not

Whether we're able,

Or whether we can.

....

The planet can look after itself.

We are not 'caring' its cause,

Just making excuses

For our common-abuses.

....

The hardest of all to manage;

Siding and abiding

By your fellow-man.

....

For every citizen

That thinks he's a hero.

Another,  feels embittered.

Each will hold his own mind's gun.

They're on a soul-mission-run.

Nothing, such as, love for all.

*Every man* thinks he's a hero.

Thank you.

Written between November 2020 and August 2021

"Grown man still acts the child;
He, full of spite that holds
The best toy in clenched hands –
Tight to his body's side."

"Look at his gluttony eyes."

"Mine!"

"Grown man's impact, as spoiled,
Wants the whole of the world,
Stamping his feet in demanding,
Everything should be mine, mine!"

"The grown men-children at tug of war,
Each wanting the argued-prize,
Each looking outward for support,
Pulling Mother Earth; the contested-ball."

"Their hands grappling its sides,
Back and forth, more and more.
They grizzle and they squawk,
Both adamant in commanding."

"Back and forth, more and more,
Breaking both their most-craved joy."

"Not acting grown-ups, matured,
Each is self-pushing their luck."

"Some to the men-playground
Stand and look, *not* playing at all.

Amongst others' sacheled-books –
As the lessons for their lives –
Through the school gates
Have sneaked a gun or knife."

"Some with spines to radicalise,
They're all viewing the leading one."

"In their wanting ploy, the short break will be destroyed."

"Dominance is each man child's thought."

....

It affects both the rich and poor.
We stand in the shiniest aura,
To dine on jealous-need.
Every person thinks they deserve more.


....

"Each may play as friendly-fun,

But never to be outdone ...

Each will choose to take sides,

... Each holding ... their own mind's gun."